Steadicam

Behind
Des &
Evelyn
as they
head to
truck

It
won't
start
Des
gets
out

crank
handle
into
hole—

still
won't
start

BRUCE BERESFORD

Josh Hartnett definitely wants to do this... true stories from a life in the screen trade

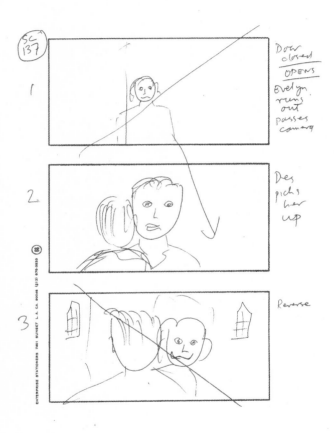

SC 137

1

Door
closed
OPENS
Evelyn
runs
out
passes
camera

2

Des
picks
her
up

3

Reverse

ENTERPRISE STATIONERS 7901 SUNSET L.A. CA 90046 (213) 876-3530

BRUCE BERESFORD

Josh Hartnett
definitely wants to
do this... true stories
from a life in the screen trade

FOURTH ESTATE • *London, New York, Sydney* and *Auckland*

Fourth Estate

An imprint of HarperCollins*Publishers*

First published in Australia in 2007
by HarperCollins*Publishers* Australia Pty Limited
ABN 36 009 913 517
www.harpercollins.com.au

HarperCollins*Publishers*

25 Ryde Road, Pymble, Sydney, NSW 2073, Australia
31 View Road, Glenfield, Auckland 10, New Zealand
77–85 Fulham Palace Road, London, W6 8JB, United Kingdom
2 Bloor Street East, 20th floor, Toronto, Ontario M4W 1A8, Canada
10 East 53rd Street, New York NY 10022, USA

National Library of Australia Cataloguing-in-Publication data:

Beresford, Bruce, 1940– .
    Josh Hartnett definitely wants to do this . . . true stories
    from a life in the screen trade.
    ISBN 13: 978 0 7322 8439 8.
    ISBN 10: 0 7322 8439 2.
    1. Motion picture industry. 2. Motion pictures – Production
    and direction. 3. Motion pictures – Australia – Production
    and direction. I. Title.
791.43

Jacket and internal design by Marcelle Lunam
Front cover photograph by Harald Staudach
All photographs are copyright of the author except where otherwise credited
Typeset in 11.5/17 Bembo by Kirby Jones
Printed and bound in Australia by Griffin Press on 80gsm Belle

5 4 3 2 1   07 08 09 10

There is no art without fanaticism . . .

—Flaubert

Bruce at 18 with a 16mm Bolex.

To Joshua and Leander

Caricature by Barry Humphries, circa 1975.

The first duty in life is to assume a pose — what the second duty is no one has yet found out.

—Oscar Wilde

INTRODUCTION

In 2003, I directed *And Starring Pancho Villa as Himself* in Mexico with Antonio Banderas in the leading role. This was made for HBO* and was meant to be filmed and edited fairly quickly, certainly much faster than a regular feature film. However, I finished up spending more time on it than on any other film I've ever made — at least 18 months. Although I had been told that the majority of TV executives were frustrated directors and prone to issuing directives demanding endless re-cuts, deletions and additions, my enthusiasm for the well-researched and exciting script by Larry Gelbart allied with my innate naïveté to ignore all warnings. About

---

* Home Box Office: a leading producer of TV series and TV movies.

two-thirds of the way through the editing process I realised I was more of an innocent bystander than a dynamic creative force. Painted into a corner, I returned to Australia, leaving the film in the capable hands of the HBO executives.

I was now able to move on to a project with which I'd been obsessed for some time — *Miss Potter*, a story about Beatrix Potter, the Victorian Englishwoman who created Peter Rabbit and other lovable vermin. The engaging, witty and rather sad script was written by a New Yorker, Richard Maltby Jnr.

Richard has directed a lot of Broadway musicals and is an accomplished songwriter who has written some of Barbra Streisand's biggest hits as well as the English lyrics for *Miss Saigon*. His original idea was to write a musical about Beatrix Potter, but for some reason he changed his mind and wrote a film script instead. When I sent the script to the Potter executors in London they were astonished that an American had so perfectly captured the manners and speech patterns of wealthy Londoners of the Victorian era. They quickly promised their full support for the project.

My enthusiasm for the script was not shared by everyone who read it — invariably the case with highly original work — but I finally aroused enough interest to find a modest budget provided a major actress was found for the leading role. I sent the script to Cate Blanchett, who more or less started her career in my film *Paradise Road*. She agreed to play Miss Potter and the film began pre-production in London. While still in Los Angeles, I had breakfast with Cate one morning and, in passing, mentioned the shooting dates. Her face clouded and she told me there must be some mistake as she wasn't available at that time.

Although in shock, I managed to cover up for another half an hour, or at least I think I did. I then rushed back to the production office and reported the conversation. It all turned out to be accurate; Cate wasn't available. I still don't know how the confusion came about. It didn't really matter. She couldn't do the film and a delay would mean the precariously balanced finance would disappear, *unless* we could find another actress acceptable to the backers. Renée Zellweger had shown interest in the past, but couldn't be pinned down; Julia Roberts, I thought, was unsuitable for the role; and no one agreed with me about Emily Watson. In fact, no one seemed to have heard of her, though only a few years ago she was all the rage because of *Breaking the Waves*, and her subsequent roles have not been negligible.*

I had no other work lined up as I'd abandoned everything for *Miss Potter*, which would have taken me a year or so to complete. I realised I would now have to resurrect some dormant projects and/or find new ones, or both. Also, it seemed I would now have time to write the script I'd been commissioned to do (at an excessively

---

* These include the Australian film *The Proposition* (2005).

Directing Antonio Banderas in *And Starring Pancho Villa as Himself.*
(Photograph by Rico Torres)

modest fee) — an adaptation of Henry Handel Richardson's three-volume novel, *The Fortunes of Richard Mahony*.

The thought struck me that it might be interesting to keep a diary of these activities, mainly to keep track of the various projects and people involved with them. (I'd made a couple of attempts at keeping diaries during various film shoots in the past, but abandoned all of them after a couple of weeks at most, mainly because I was always too exhausted at night to be bothered by writing about the day.)

I never thought about publication until recently. I was checking through some old notes and found them quite amusing. It occurred to me it might be of interest for people to read about the difficulties of setting up films rather than chronicles of them being made.

I've always found published diaries and letters quite fascinating, even those that were so uneventful they didn't do much more than provide a list of meals and occasional meetings with passers-by. I recently read a passage by Anatole France that explained this obsession. 'We complain that people talk about themselves, yet it is a subject they treat better than any other. A writer is rarely so well inspired as when he is telling his own story . . . we must bear in mind that there is in all of us a positive need for truth which at times impels us to reject all fiction, however beautiful. We all enjoy the private letters and the notebooks of great men, and even of little men, provided they have

. . . left a little of their inner selves at the point of their pen. We enjoy all confessions and all reminiscences. Writers never bore us by writing of their loves and their hates, their joys and their sorrows . . .'*

---

* Sacha Guitry, *If I Remember Right: Memoirs of Sacha Guitry*, London: Methuen & Co Ltd, 1935. First English edition. Translated from the French by Lewis Galantiere.

24th October 2003

A script arrives, via email (they nearly all do these days), written by the notorious Jeffrey Archer, bestselling novelist and once Chairman of the Conservative Party, who was given my address by the art dealer Philip Bacon.

Curious, I read it straight away. *Walking Off the Map* is about the British climber George Mallory, who attempted Everest in 1924. He may have reached the top and died on the way down (evidently going down mountains is far more risky than going up them), but no one knows if he was the first to reach the summit. His body was found, perfectly preserved, if rather battered from the fall which caused his death, in 1999, by an American group of climbers. Evidently they were tipped off about the location of the body by a member of a Chinese expedition who had attempted Everest a couple of years previously. It was hoped that Mallory's camera would be in one of his pockets with the film still undeveloped. This could show if the summit had been reached. However, there was no camera. It's still not been found and probably never will be.

The script is well written. Clearly a lot of research has been done. (I assume Jeffrey Archer had plenty of time to do this while he was in gaol for two years for perjury.) There is a lot of fascinating detail about the organisation of the Everest expedition and the personalities involved. News to me was that Mallory's favoured climbing partner was the Australian Charles Finch, father of the actor Peter Finch. Mallory regarded Finch as the world's best climber, but was told by the Royal Geographic Society he could not take him on the Everest attempt (which would be Mallory's second try at the mountain) because (a) he — Finch — had failed to pay his bar bill (evidently only a couple of pounds); (b) he was a divorced man; and, worst of all, (c) he was an Australian. Mallory was given a far less experienced climber (Andrew Irvine) as a partner and the script raises the question whether the team of Mallory and Finch, rather than Mallory and Irvine, would have reached the summit in 1924, many years before the successful Edmund Hillary and Norgay Tensing expedition.

These days, just about anyone (with enough money) can climb Everest up a well-marked trail, but in Mallory's day no one knew what the best route would be. It's hard to believe, too, that the climbers were wearing three-piece tweed suits and had equipment that would be comical today for a climb up Kosciuszko.

With some trepidation, I phoned Jeffrey Archer and told him how much I liked the script. He was affable and quite happy to receive any notes I cared to send.

How many scripts have I read in the past 25 years? Hundreds. Solicited and unsolicited, I'm happy to read them all, even if some lay around for months while I try to find time. I feel an obligation to the writers, virtually all of whom have put in a vast amount of work, even if little talent is discernible in the final result. A more important reason is a selfish one. There might be a gem among the material. In a few cases, very few, I've either made the film (*Tender Mercies*), or encouraged the writer to keep trying and/or advised him/her of someone who could be interested in their work. There is no fee ever involved, even if the scripts come from a studio and my notes take a week or more to compile.

25th October 2003

Met with Sue Milliken* at her office in Fox Studios, Sydney, to discuss, again, the possibility of finding financial

---

* Producer of my films *Paradise Road* (1997), *The Fringe Dwellers* (1986) and *Black Robe* (1991) as well as others, including *The Odd Angry Shot* (1979) and *Sirens* (1994).

backing for *The Women in Black*.* The details of finance are quite beyond me and I have a habit of nodding off as money and contracts are mentioned. It seems there is a London company interested in putting up 5% of the budget. This seems very very little. It is, in fact, very very little. We'll have to approach the Film Finance Corporation for investment as well. I am depressed at the prospect of this as it always seems to be the case that the scripts I am most enthusiastic about are the same ones that investors disparage.

The (possible) English investors are definitely enthusiastic about the script, fortunately, though it has been stressed to us that we must find 'name' actors. (This seems to be *de rigueur* these days even for low-budget films.) They are excited to hear that we sent the script to Isabella Rossellini for the role of the migrant, Magda, and that Isabella thought the role superb. No wonder. It is. All the same I doubt if any American backers (and we'll need them) will throw their hats in the air, or their money at us, because of her. We'll need a 'name' Australian actor to play the dad. Geoffrey Rush would be perfect, maybe Sam Neill, maybe Bryan Brown, though he seems to mostly do mini-series these days. Not much point in

---

* From the novel by Madeleine St John. A charming story set in 1960 in a David Jones type department store. Sue and I co-wrote the script a couple of years ago.

approaching any of them until the money looks a bit more likely ...

Came home and continued working on script of *The Fortunes of Richard Mahony*. Very difficult to adapt as the novel, probably longer than *Gone With the Wind* or *War and Peace*, rambles quite a lot. I'm sure I'm one of the very few people who has read the whole thing, at least since it was published around 1930. Atmospheric and undeniably powerful,* and a well-observed main character (a portrait of Richardson's father), *Richard Mahony* has very little plot but numerous irrelevancies and loads of unnecessary characters. She (Ethel Richardson wrote under the name Henry Handel Richardson) really needed a good editor, as she often drops characters then invents new ones who perform the same function. Why not keep the original characters and provide more continuity? It must be at least partially because the three volumes were published separately with some years between them. The first two sold so badly that Richardson was forced to publish the concluding volume herself. Luckily, it was then combined with the first two and became a bestseller through the 1930s. The third volume, Mahony on the downhill track to insanity, is the most gripping, probably because Richardson, as a child, was able to observe her

---

* The story of an Irish doctor who emigrates to the Victorian goldfields in the mid-19th century, and his subsequent fortunes.

father's decline. I know this gloomy ending is going to be a problem with backers. Tragic endings often work superbly (tragedy often has an exhilarating quality) — virtually all operas end with the lovers separated or dead — but film financiers want the conventional happy fade out. Amazing that *Gone With the Wind*, still the biggest moneymaker ever, has an ending where the hero walks away from the heroine.

26th October 2003

Tried to find if there are other scripts of *Richard Mahony*. In the 1930s, when the novel was a huge success, MGM announced more than once that they were filming it. Presumably someone wrote a screenplay? Very hard to track it down now but I want to be prepared if someone springs up and claims authorship of the screenplay. Script writers are notoriously litigious and the Writers Guild notoriously eccentric in their adjudications over screen credit. I remember the fiasco of the *King David* credits. Andrew Birkin* wrote the script, but it turned out a writer named James Costigan had written a *King David* screenplay some years previously. The Writers Guild

---

* Brother of English singer and actress Jane Birkin. He has written or co-written a number of films, including *The Name of the Rose* (1986) and *The Messenger* (1999).

adjudicated that Birkin had to share credit — on the basis that the same characters (Saul, Bathsheba, etc) and some of the same incidents bobbed up in both versions! I told them at the time, in a deposition, that this was clearly inevitable. They took no notice.

I remember, too, that John Morris wanted to make *Richard Mahony* when he ran the South Australian Film Corporation in the 1970s. That came to nothing and I don't think he had a script written. Later, Dino De Laurentiis talked about doing it, but, again, no script was commissioned. I think he looked at the 1000-page book and considered it too formidable.

There has been a radio adaptation, I'm told, and a stage play. I've not seen or read either. It would make a great opera. It has all the ingredients — a great love story, superb roles for tenor, baritone and soprano and a *de rigueur* tragic ending.

27th October 2003

Script arrives from a producer in London, Sheryl Crown. *The Dead Wait*, written by a South African named Paul Herzberg and adapted from his own play. A strong story, with only three major characters. Set during the war in Angola, it has two South African soldiers, one a very young recruit, who capture an African rebel leader and decide to carry him (as he's wounded) back to their own lines. Pursued by the African's forces, a relationship develops between the three men.

A call from Mark Pennell* to say that *Boswell for the Defence*† has been resurrected. Can I go to London to sign production papers, meet the new line producer and possibly go on a location survey to Latvia? Latvia! Cheaper to shoot there than in London. I'm not even going to mention this to my Hollywood agent; I know what he'll say — he warned me off the project in the first place. He insisted the finance was dubious. Infuriatingly, he turned out to be correct.

29th October 2003

Sheryl Crown insists she can find the finance for *The Dead Wait*, partially from South Africa, and that Colin Firth is interested in playing one of the soldiers. Wants me to go to London to discuss. She says, somewhat unconvincingly, that if I pay for the fare over I will be reimbursed.

The trip might be worthwhile all the same. Could it be true that *Boswell* is going to be made after all? Anyway,

---

* An ex-actor (*Neighbours*) and one of the three producers on the ill-fated *Boswell for the Defence* (1981), written by Patrick Edgeworth.

† A film based on the true story of how the drunken James Boswell, long after his days of glory as the biographer of Samuel Johnson, had the unenviable job of defending Mary Broad in the London courts after her escape from the New South Wales penal colony.

I can meet the people re *The Women in Black*, and Jeffrey Archer.

2nd November 2003

Flew to London on Emirates. They have cheap flights for people over 60! Depressing. Sat next to a Canadian girl dressed in T-shirt and shorts who has been on holiday in Australia for a month. She works in catering at an oil drilling plant in the Yemen where there are 6000 men and six women. All sorts of questions sprang to mind, but she was so earnest I thought it inadvisable to ask any of them.

Arrived at my Bloomsbury flat around midday. The tenants are away and agreed I could use it for a week. All I'd asked, begged, them to do was to remember to close the living room curtains at night as the early morning sun (on the odd days that it shines) hits my precious (valuable?) collection of pictures and can fade them. The curtains are wide open. Also, the TV, video and stereo don't work, nor does the hot water tap in the bathroom. At least these people pay the rent regularly, unlike the previous three tenants, none of whom paid anything. One of them, an American lawyer, a woman, even insisted on having her deposit back (despite the fact it was all she'd ever paid), a request issued with the threat 'if you don't return it I'll bring in someone to smash the place up'. The agent who handled the rental insisted she must be bluffing, but what if she wasn't? Terrified of my precious Brangwyns* and Rippl-Rónai† being slashed — I returned the deposit.

3rd November 2003

Went with film lawyer Carlo Dusi, a very anglicised Italian, to a meeting with Hilary Davis at Beyond Films. She reiterated her enthusiasm for *The Women in Black* and thinks they can raise some finance. They'll need to pre-sell it to two countries at least. 'Isn't it the case,' I asked, 'that the various European countries these days tend to only put up some money once they've *seen* the film, not at script stage? So they're likely to be no help at all with financing?' Yes, I was told, this does tend to be the pattern. In his clipped, precise English, Carlo said all we could do is try.

Dinner at Sheekey's with Sheryl Crown (producer), Paul Herzberg (writer) and Colin Firth (potential leading man) to discuss *The Dead Wait*. Colin is clearly keen to play the main role of a tough South African soldier, as it will be a major change of pace from all the light comedies he's been making. It turns out he's just been to a crew

---

* Frank Brangwyn (1867–1956). A prolific British painter with a brilliant sense of composition and flair for colour. Now almost forgotten, with a revival regularly being predicted, his works fetched higher prices than Picasso until the early 1930s.

† Józef Rippl-Rónai (1861–1927). A gifted Hungarian figurative painter. I have only one drawing of his, purchased at a market in Los Angeles about 20 years ago.

screening of his new film, *Love Actually*. Says he thought it was hopeless while it was being made but was pleasantly surprised at the final edit.

We say goodnight in the laneway outside. I suspect Sheryl had to stretch to pay for the dinner and I feel a bit guilty I didn't contribute (London restaurant prices are so high I'm always stunned at the number of patrons — what can they all be doing for a living, that they can afford to eat in these places?), but console myself with the thought that she'd told me while I was in Sydney that the film was financed — around $8 million — and I should come to London to meet everyone. It's obvious it isn't financed. Partially perhaps, but that's all. I don't think that air fare is going to be reimbursed, either. Still, if I don't invest some time and effort in projects I like I'll never make any films at all. Great scripts like *Tender Mercies* and *Driving Miss Daisy* just arrived in the post (pre email) and it took a lot of work to get them into production.

Colin and I walk up into Tottenham Court Road. We've met a few times before as we had a mutual friend in the Irish writer Brian Moore.* Colin asks if I think Sheryl can pull the film together. I tell him I was about to ask him the same thing. I find we both think her endless phone calls are over-verbose but very short on real

---

* Author of *Black Robe*, *The Lonely Passion of Judith Hearne* and many other works.

information. She's well-intentioned without a doubt, but getting the finance for a film outside the studio system is mountainously difficult. The stars have to be locked in before anyone will put up any money and the stars usually won't read the scripts unless the money is in place. Sheryl has reached first base in having a relatively major star show interest.

5th November 2003

In Soho, Sheryl Crown and I climb endless flights of stairs to the office of a casting director, a friendly, direct and very large woman. Why is this the norm with casting directors? It seems to be as standard as the law that requires fashion designers to have shapeless figures, which they drape in the most styleless clothes imaginable.

We won't get *The Dead Wait* off the ground with Colin Firth alone. There are only two other parts — an African guerrilla fighter (black) and a young South African recruit (white). I'm in favour of casting South African actors in the interests of authenticity, but am told there are none with a 'name' except, possibly, Richard E. Grant and he's too old and too suave for one role, and the wrong colour for the other. For the guerrilla fighter someone suggests Djimon Hounsou, who has a major role in Jim Sheridan's *In America* and was in

Amistad. At least he's a genuine African. A call is made to Hounsou's agent in Los Angeles; he is told the script will be sent. For the young soldier the names of various English actors are kicked around. Sheryl tells us that Joseph Fiennes has read the part and is enthusiastic, but adds that the finance people don't think too highly of him. The 'finance people' are a menace these days. An elusive group, invariably uncontactable, and prone to omnipotent pronouncements about which actors are and are not suitable for roles. I doubt if these decisions are ever made on a reading of the script, but simply relate to 'marketability'. Directors regularly recoil in horror as actors are suggested to them that they know are wildly unsuitable for a particular role. A few years ago I was forced to drop Emmanuelle Seigneur (Roman Polanski's wife and a fine actress) from the lead role of *Bride of the Wind* on the basis that 'European audiences don't like her'. I was never shown any proof of this accusation and those European audiences seem to have endured her presence in a number of successful films.

Then a visit to the Film Council. A chic office in Little Portland Street. Sheryl insists they will invest in the film. I'm not so convinced. They are polite but rather formal and make noises about script changes. I tell them that Paul Herzberg is working on a revised draft from my notes.

Evening. I go to The Caprice to meet Jeffrey Archer for the first time.

The Caprice along with its sister restaurant, The Ivy, are two of my favourite restaurants in the world. They're no more expensive than most London eating houses — which is very expensive — but the food, basically superbly cooked school dinners, is excellent. It's great to be able to order bangers and mash, or haddock and squashed peas, bubble and squeak, spotted dick, bread pudding and all those dishes so frowned on by the chefs of modern haute cuisine, cookery writers and weight watchers. The Ivy, I know, takes bookings up to a year ahead, BUT celebrities can get in without any problem. Ever since *Driving Miss Daisy*, I've found a table quite easy to get, even though the film had terrible reviews and failed dismally at the box office in England. Celebrity, even minor celebrity, has some perks, though I recall Edward Woodward* telling me there is a downside. 'Sometimes it's the best tables,' he said, 'plus a rapid move through queues at airports, but it often results in an anal search from some crabby Customs officer, intent on humiliating the successful.'

I've barely entered the crowded bar area when a man approaches, saying, 'Ah, Lord Archer's guest.' How could he have known? I'm not an actor, nor a famous face, and hadn't said anything, so my Australian accent couldn't have given me away. I'm aware of the hierarchy of tables at The Caprice and not that surprised when I'm guided to a table by the window, which I know is the No. 1 spot.

---

* English actor. Played the eponymous role in *Breaker Morant* (1980).

Jeffrey Archer, a trim-looking man of average height with eyes described by the authors of bodice rippers as 'sparkling', is one of those people whose relaxed and direct manner immediately puts everyone at their ease. I had heard a lot of scandal about him, but the biography I'd read didn't really come up with anything substantial. I think his gaol sentence, four years, was rather severe when basically he had lied in court while covering up a liaison with a lady. Most of my friends could be in gaol on this basis — though he provided ammunition for his political enemies (he was Chairman of the Tory party at the time) by suing a newspaper for libel over the case. He won, but then had to recant when it turned out that appointments in a diary had been fabricated and friends persuaded to say he was dining with them when he was otherwise engaged.

Denying affairs is always advisable, I have been assured. An actor friend of mine told me that he even produced an explanation on an occasion when his wife caught him in the act. He calmly stated that the lady underneath him on the floor had fallen backwards and he was merely trying to help her up off the slippery floorboards (which accounted for the *appearance* of intercourse) when the wife entered the room. I am not sure that the wife was gullible enough to accept this as entirely plausible.

I have no problem enthusing about the script of *Walking Off the Map*. I have a few suggestions for alterations, though I'd need to know a lot more about mountain climbing (not a sport I am addicted to) before I could be of much help.

Jeffrey chats quite frankly about his two years or so in gaol. It wasn't much fun, but he managed to capitalise on it. The three volumes of his *Prison Diaries* are not only bestsellers, but the only success he's had with literary critics. The style is simple and direct, without a touch of self-pity as it effortlessly brings tedious prison routine and colourful characters to life.

Quite a few people pause by our table. All are very courteous and address Jeffrey as 'Lord Archer' (a title the Blair government is arranging to remove). I get the feeling they think the abuse he has had in the press and his gaol sentence were excessive.

6th November 2003

At the Groucho Club in Soho I meet David Wicht,* the South African co-producer of *The Dead Wait*. Tall, handsome and affable, he enthuses about South African crews, but is vague about the amount of finance that he can find toward the $8 million budget.

The Groucho is the major hangout for film people. Next, I see Rainer Mockert, one of the three 'producers' of *Boswell for the Defence*, the film I worked on for 14 months only to have it cancelled eight days from the beginning of

---

* Produced numerous South African films and TV series. He wrote and directed a feature, *Windprints* (1990), with John Hurt and Sean Bean.

photography with the explanation — delivered in a 20-second mobile phone call — that there was 'no money'. I repeat to him my information from Mark Pennell — that the money has been found again and that the contract can be signed. (Rumours of the film resurfacing have been hinted at for over two years and I've not paid much attention, but this time it seems like it could happen.)

Hmmmm . . . Rainer is as charming as ever. Always a bad sign. 'Ze contract,' he says, 'can be signed in two weeks.' What can I do? I tell him I'd planned to go to Boston to see my son, so I suppose I could go now instead of later. This will be fine, he assures me, 'we can sign it when you return'.

I go to Jeffrey Archer's embankment apartment. Almost opposite the Houses of Parliament, it has amazing views up and down the Thames. There is a vast art collection including four Rupert Bunny paintings and 11 by John Glover. He is impressed by my ability to name the various painters. Finally, he produces a small painted sculpture and asks me to identify the sculptor, adding that no one so far has successfully done so. Rapidly, I say 'Eric Gill'. Quite right, but not too astounding, as I've just finished reading a well-illustrated biography of Gill.

We go to the Tate Gallery for lunch with an elderly lady named Audrey Salkind — an expert on all things Everest. She has climbed most of the way up the mountain herself, has written books on George Mallory and knew many members of the expeditions of the 1920s. I know from researching previous films that, no matter how arcane the subject, there will be a handful of people who know everything there is to know. The Boer War seemed to engage the most fanatical. While researching *Breaker Morant* I met an obsessed group — the intense Welsh actor Kenneth Griffith* among them — whose entire houses were nothing less than Boer War shrines, every room littered with Boer War paraphenalia; medals, weapons, flags, photographs, books, etc. The conversation of these people could deal tediously and pedantically with every battle, every troop manoeuvre, every ribbon, every medal. After the film was released I was attacked by an Australian fanatic who told me that a medal Lord Kitchener was wearing was incorrect. I countered by producing a photograph showing Kitchener wearing the medal. 'Aha!' was the triumphant response, 'he only wore it when being photographed. Never at any other time.' My riposte was that he was being photographed for the film so the medal was correct.

Back at the luxury embankment apartment I introduce Jeffrey to my London agent Steve Kenis, and the producer Sarah Radclyffe. It's clear that Jeffrey thinks, mistakenly we all know, that it will be quite easy to raise the $50 million or so that we'll need to make the film. The story, he points out, is quite extraordinary and he has our assurance that he's done a great job on the script. All true, BUT this

---

* Kenneth Griffith (1921–2006) made dozens of films. Best known for *I'm All Right Jack* (1959) and *A Night to Remember* (1958).

doesn't mean everyone, or even anyone, is going to agree. First, I tell him, we'll have to get a major actor attached so that the Hollywood studios will see some commercial potential. I tell Jeffrey that the studio heads won't read the script so we must have a 'package' that appeals. We try to think of suitable actors — Jude Law, Ewan McGregor, Christian Bale, Paul Bettany . . . Jeffrey has no doubt that all of them will leap at the role of George Mallory.

7th November 2003

Spend the whole day in the flat going through the script of *The Dead Wait* with Paul Herzberg. I've now read his stage play, which was the basis of the film script. There are a few things that could be included and I tell him I think some of the soldiers' philosophising may have worked on stage but will be very artificial on film. The chase aspect, as the South African soldiers make their way to the border with their rebel captive, can be more detailed, more tense, more exciting. I suspect Paul thinks I am torpedoing his fine writing.

8th November 2003

Decided on the spur of the moment to fly to Italy to see Jeffrey Smart. A mini-cab to Stansted airport at 3 am!

Jeffrey Smart at work in his studio.

The flight leaves at 6.30 am and I'm told the security measures are equivalent to those at the White House so to be there at 4.30. Not surprisingly, the security measures are minimal and by 5.00 am I'm sitting in the departure lounge with a large group of miserable, tired-looking Brits all on their way to a holiday in Florence. A two-hour flight to Pisa. I rent a car and drive three hours down the autostrada to Arezzo. Haven't been here for a few years but somehow remember the turnoff, thus saving myself a 40-mile trip to the next exit. After that it's about another 10 miles or so over minor roads to the tiny village of Presciano, Tuscany, where Jeffrey has lived for at least 30 years.

The whole area has been built up since my last visit. There is even a row of townhouses on the outskirts of the village.

The property has security gates. I buzz and they slowly open. The house is an old farmhouse, heavily restored, with the cattle cleared out of the ground floor (now the guest room), central heating installed, the kitchen turned into the living room, the verandah glassed in — and so on.

As I expected, Jeffrey is at work in his studio. I know he won't come out until the evening. I put my bag in the guest room and cross the courtyard to the converted pigeon coop, where he is working on a large painting dominated by a huge stretch of highway. At the top of the picture is a row of small motel rooms. I know that people are often astonished that he could live in such a picturesque part of Italy and yet paint mostly modern buildings and roads, with an occasional human figure lost somewhere in the composition. Yet these images dominate the lives of all of us, in nearly every country, so it has never surprised me that at least one painter would respond to these fascinating visual aspects of the 20th and 21st centuries.

He greets me affably, adding 'sit behind me so you won't distract me and we can talk'. Classical music blares out from a new digital station, broadcasting from London. 'Why don't they play more Delius?' he moans, adding — 'Can you send them an email and find out why?' I watch him carefully adding brush strokes to his meticulously constructed composition and talk about my various film projects. I know he watches a lot of new films on DVD though prefers those of the 1930s and 40s, with a particular penchant for Marlene Dietrich. He knows all of her songs off by heart and sings them with a reasonable imitation of her German accent, emphasising her inability to pronounce 'w'.

After dinner, Jeffrey and I watch an early 1930s Marlene Dietrich film, *Dishonoured*. It's directed by Josef von Sternberg* so has moody and contrasty lighting (by Lee Garmes), but a plot of outstanding absurdity in which Dietrich, playing a prostitute, is recruited by the Austrian secret service to spy on Russian soldiers. She ends up

---

* (1894–1969) He may have been born in Austria but grew up in the USA. The 'von' was added when he went to Hollywood.

falling for a Russian officer, played by the totally miscast Victor McLaglen* (far too old, cumbersome and just plain ugly for the part), lets him escape — he only has to climb out of a window and seems to be back in Moscow — and is executed in the final scene.

Von Sternberg virtually ruined Dietrich's career with a string of these films throughout the 30s. She was finally rescued by the success of *Destry Rides Again*, a 1939 western with James Stewart.

Ermes De Zan, Jeffrey's partner, correctly predicted the film would be rubbish and went to bed. Jeffrey complained that he only likes to watch animal documentaries.

9th November 2003

A cold and wet day. I spend a couple of hours walking in the hills behind the house. Ermes tells me there is an Etruscan road going through the trees and the paving stones can still be seen. I find nothing, but stumble across an old and well-kept walled cemetery. Most of the graves have fresh flowers and many have photographs of the deceased.

Spend the remainder of the day reading through a pile of scripts that were sent to the flat in London. Nothing exciting.

---

* Victor McLaglen (1886–1959) won an Academy Award in John Ford's *The Informer* (1935).

Again, I call into the studio and watch Jeffrey adding detail to his already detailed painting. I have always been impressed by his work ethic. No matter what the distractions, no matter who is visiting, he paints at least six hours a day, seven days a week. Not bad for a man in his eighties. He makes me feel lazy. I know that Bach said that anyone could be as successful as him (Bach, not Jeffrey) if they worked hard enough. That couldn't be true, talent has to be a factor, but sheer application to the job definitely pays off.

At dusk, Jeffrey asks if I'd like to go with him to a local pharmacists to pick up a few things. Hermes says it would be far better if I drive, but Jeffrey defends his driving skills. He likes driving. (I remember my father did, too, but I took away his car after he managed to drive it into the Hawkesbury River with my mother and a friend of hers as passengers.)

On the way to the village with the pharmacy, a few miles away, we go through the narrow streets of Presciano. The car scrapes noisily against stone walls on both sides, though Jeffrey appears not to notice. When we leave the pharmacy, which is on a steep hill and blind corner, he backs the car out so that it blocks the road for some minutes. Tension mounts as I watch the corner for an approaching vehicle. All clear. Sheer luck.

Evening. We go to dinner with some Americans, Robert and Beverly Katz, who live only a mile or so away — again, in a beautifully restored old farmhouse. The whole of Tuscany is full of expatriates (the British call it

'Chiantishire') — from England, America, Australia, France, etc. Most of them seem to know one another. Bob Katz must now be around 70. He and his wife have lived here for as long as Jeffrey. Bob is a writer,* so can, like Jeffrey, live anywhere he wants, a choice made even easier with the onslaught of computers. This evening he's excited — a 20-year-old script of his (*The Shooter*) has been picked up by some producer and is to be filmed with Wesley Snipes and Lena Headey.

After a few bottles of wine and prompted by talk of the marital problems of one of the Katz sons, Jeffrey offers the view that masturbation is far preferable to the complexities of taking out ladies. There is, he points out, no need to book tables or buy flowers or chocolates or wine or get involved in tedious conversations that one sustains in the hope of some sex at the end of the evening. Satisfaction can be achieved alone, free of complications.

11th November 2003

London. Jasmin Prosser arrives at my flat. While I was still in Australia she sent me a script about a World War II spy named Popov. The script, I thought, had far too much

---

* His best known film scripts are *The Cassandra Crossing* (1976) and *Massacre in Rome* (1973). His best known book is his biography of the German director Werner Fassbinder.

dialogue and appeared to be a translation so that the dialogue, although clear enough, didn't actually contain any sentences that a native English speaker would actually say.

Jasmin is a glamorous Croatian ex-model, tall, with fluent English. Perhaps more verbose than fluent, she pauses only to light one cigarette after another. She confirms that the script is a translation from Croatian and sees no problem with the dialogue. I try to point out the difference between lines that can be understood and lines that capture actual speech patterns; a distinction of no interest to her. She launches into an elaborate but impenetrable explanation of the financing, the core of which seems to be that she already has $60 million to make the film.

Pleading, truthfully, financial naïveté, I take her around to Steve Kenis' office in Dean Street and leave them alone. She is already chatting rapidly and smoking as I make my escape.

Steve calls me about an hour later and in his laconic Californian style tells me 'she doesn't have a fuckin' bean'. Jasmin is now added to my list of deluded would-be-producers.

12th November 2003

Lunch with the novelist William Boyd and his French producer friend, Xavier Marchand, re the adaptation of Will's novel, *The Blue Afternoon*. Again, it's a matter of casting the leading female role. I think we're experiencing resistance because none of them relish the sequence where they are packed naked in ice as a ploy for the lovers to escape from the Philippines. (The story, set around 1900, is, like so many novels, acceptable on the page, but may have plausibility problems as a movie. On the other hand, do audiences worry about this?)

Evening. A preview of a mountain climbing film, *Touching the Void*, directed by Kevin Macdonald. Done in documentary style, it recreates (with actors I assume) an actual climb in the Andes. Easily the best climbing sequences ever filmed. A lot of it must have been done in the studio, but it's impossible to spot it. I'm used to all these mountain films looking horribly phoney, painted backdrops of mountains just don't work . . . *Black Narcissus** (an absurd story — how could it have such a reputation?) was shot entirely at Pinewood Studios and has painted mountains quite obviously hanging just a few feet behind the actors. *The Mountain*† with Spencer Tracy, has rear-projection that similarly fails to create any atmosphere at all. Tracy must be the least convincing mountaineer of all time. He doesn't look like he could climb up a flight of short steps.

Walking Off the Map would have to be done this well. *Touching the Void* has raised the bar.

---

* Directed by Michael Powell (1947), with Deborah Kerr and David Farrar.

† Directed by Edward Dmytryk (1956).

Had a drink in an almost pitch-black bar in Knightsbridge with Australian producer and financier James Vernon, who is over here from Sydney seeing people about his script, *Tent Hill Road*. It's a good story — about an unsolved triple murder in Queensland in 1898. Again, without some big stars the budget will be hard to find. Jeremy Irons is interested, but will his name help? James explains to me, at great length, how the British tax laws work. I have absolutely no understanding whatever of what he's talking about. I hope he has some idea.

The martinis are no good. They seem so simple. Why can't anyone make them outside America? But then Americans can't make tea and it's only a matter of pouring boiling water over tea leaves.

13th November 2003

To Paris on the Eurostar. Train is great, three hours to Paris is quicker than a flight once all the time wasted on check-ins is counted. Food on board is truly abysmal. Ghastly stale sandwiches and lukewarm tea. Why don't the French take care of the food?

I meet Benjamin* for a couple of days sightseeing. We stay at a very modest hotel, the Odessa near Montparnasse.

---

* My son. He lives in Normandy with his mother, my ex-wife, Rhoisin (pronounced 'Roo-sheen').

I drag him off to a number of galleries, including a few obscure ones — the Gallery of Romantic Art, Brancusi's studio, and Victor Hugo's house. His interest is limited, but he politely follows along knowing that at some point there will be a steak *avec frites* and, possibly, a movie. Despite some years in France his French is very limited, though he has no problem ordering food and drinks. My French is limited despite years of study. I can speak moderately well but have absolutely no idea what anyone is saying to me. I'm sure even the French have problems. I've read that the words for 'under' (*au-dessous de*) and 'above' (*au-dessus de*) sound so similar that French fighter pilots were constantly flying into each other during the war as the words were so easy to confuse over the radio.

In a poster shop near Notre Dame I find a huge poster for Fellini's *Il Bidone*,* one of my favourite films. It was considered disappointing after *La Strada*, but this could have been because it tells a harrowing story of two men who travel around the country impersonating priests and conning money out of peasants with an elaborate story of jewellery hidden on their farms during the war. Broderick Crawford gives perhaps his best performance, though he runs it a close second in *All The Kings Men* and *The Fastest Gun Alive*.

Benjamin and I argue for some time about which movie to go and see. I finally win, regrettably, with *The Human Stain*. Adapted from the novel by Philip Roth,

---

* Aka *The Swindlers* (1955).

With my son, Benjamin, on the set of *And Starring Pancho Villa as Himself*.
(Photograph by Rico Torres)

this is probably the least successful effort from Robert
Benton — a gifted writer/director.* Nicole Kidman is
totally miscast as a cleaning lady (!) and Anthony
Hopkins as an African–American! There are even
misjudged flashback sequences with another actor,
who bears no resemblance whatever, playing him as a
younger man.

17th November 2003

Back in the Groucho Club. I meet Joseph Fiennes
and Cillian Murphy, both for *The Dead Wait*. Fiennes is
clearly interested and would be ideal, but I've already
been told 'the financiers don't like him' . . . Murphy is
almost unknown but everyone says he's on the verge
of a breakthrough. Odd how word gets around about
some actors even though they've barely been seen. I
remember it was the same a few years ago with Cate
Blanchett, and international stardom was confidently
predicted for Mel Gibson when he was still a student
at NIDA.

I think Cillian Murphy feels a small film like *The
Dead Wait* might be a waste of time with Hollywood
about to call.

---

* Robert Benton did an uncredited script polish on *Double Jeopardy* (1999).

Called Alan Bates,* who is in hospital with cancer. 'This isn't much fun,' he said. He didn't seem keen for me to visit him, so I fear the worst. I mumbled something about seeing him when I come back to England next year. Both of us know he won't be around.

18th November 2003

Visit Madeleine St John, who I've known since we were at university. She lives in a top-floor flat in Notting Hill, with a vicious cat that snarls and snaps at visitors. She has published four novels. One of them, *The Essence of the Thing*, was nominated for the Booker Prize. I have to tell her that I've still not found the finance to film her first novel, *The Women in Black*. She affects indifference, but I know it must be bitterly disappointing. She has emphysema, is almost permanently on oxygen and is so frail that I imagine that every visit I make will be the last. She doesn't complain, is as witty as ever, and we arrange to go to a concert at the Albert Hall.

Evening. Met Michael Fitzgerald at the Groucho Club. A charming Irish–American who produced *Mister Johnson*, a film we made in Nigeria in 1990, with Pierce Brosnan.

---

* Outstanding British actor, famous for *Women in Love* (1969), *The Go Between* (1970) and many other films. I thought Alan should have been nominated in my film *Evelyn* (2002).

Michael only ever paid me a fraction of the agreed fee, but didn't hesitate to point out, when we were interviewed together on TV in New York, that he still thought I had earned too much on the film. A few years ago he formed a company with the actor Sean Penn. After one successful film in 2001, *The Pledge*, directed by Penn, the company broke up and he's now making a film about a Stanley Kubrick impersonator, *Colour me Kubrick*.* Michael affects a great knowledge of the intricacies of film financing, though I'm not entirely convinced of his expertise. The crew were often waiting for their salaries during the production of *Mister Johnson* and I recall his strange sudden trips from Nigeria to . . . where? Probably London or New York. Somehow, admittedly, Michael always returned with enough to pay everyone — except me. He is invariably brimming with self-confidence, an aspect of character that causes me anxiety. Michael at one stage went to Nigeria without a visa, assuring me that this would not be a problem. A couple of days in a gaol in Kano disabused him of this.

21st November 2003

Went with Madeleine St John to the concert at the Albert Hall. Mitsuko Uchida plays the Schumann Piano

---

* This film was released in 2006.

Concerto. Quite an ordeal getting the frail Madeleine out of the taxi then along the side of the hall and finally up to our seats on the side. Madeleine adored the performance. She is disparaging about most pianists, but worships Uchida. Interestingly, she seems to know as much about jazz — Art Tatum being her favourite — as she does about classical music. It depresses me that of my children only Cordelia likes classical music. The others — as well as my sister's three children — all seem to regard it as fuddy-duddy stuff, an opinion I find impossible to understand. I remember finding it so appealing when I first heard a broadcast* on the ABC classical station when I was around 15. It was always difficult to listen to music in our house at Toongabbie,† where I spent so much of my childhood. My father hated noise of any kind, so he forbade the radio being turned on. He once made me give away a beloved cat on the grounds that its pawsteps, as it padded around the house, disturbed him.

Strange that dislike of classical music can be so virulent. Jeffrey Smart told me recently that the classical FM station in Florence was taken off the air by the new Communist mayor on the grounds it was 'elitist'. A strange claim when anyone can listen without charge. In a biography of Stalin (who had a good singing voice,

---

* It was Tchaikovsky's 'Capriccio Italien'.

† In the western suburbs of Sydney.

but preferred folk songs to anything classical), I read that he had plans to shut down the Russian ballet, but then withdrew them when he found out they were almost the only group in Moscow who supported him politically.

Among my many unrealised projects is an adaptation of David Edgar's play *Master Class* (to be produced by the New Zealander Bill Gavin) in which Stalin torments Prokofiev and Shostakovich, urging them to use more folk tunes in order that their music is more accessible. Incredible that the leader of such a vast empire could be bothered spending so much of his time over such an issue. No doubt the acclaim these composers had in the West is the only reason they both didn't end up in Siberia.

22nd November 2003

Boston. Adam* meets me at the airport. We go straight to a coffee shop where I tell him it's crucial we see the Australia–England rugby final, which takes place in a few hours. It won't be on TV here. A man at a nearby table leans over and gives us the address of an Irish pub where the game can be seen.

---

* My son. Adam gained a PhD in Classics from Balliol College, Oxford, and is now in the Philosophy department at the University of Massachusetts.

That evening I don't think we'll get in. The pub is crowded, but we find two great seats near one of the huge screens. Every Brit in town is present. England wins a terrific game.

23rd November 2003

Peter Weir's film *Master and Commander*. Superbly directed and with a characteristically flawless performance from Russell Crowe. I never much cared for those Patrick O'Brian novels as they seem to be all descriptions of boats and how to tie knots and no plot. The film tries to escape this by combining a few of the novels, though there still isn't much of a story. I prefer the *Sharpe* novels by Bernard Cornwall, though, as Adam points out, all of those have exactly the *same* plot.

Go with Adam and a Cameroonian friend of his, a political philosopher named Azume, to a very smart restaurant. I'm looking jet lagged and tired, Adam is dressed like a tramp, down to shoes that don't constitute a pair. Only Azume, a handsome man, is well dressed with a jacket and tie. The hostess hesitates at the sight of us, though is partially reassured by Azume. 'Do you have a reservation?' she asks. Adam replies, 'No, we like it here.' She doesn't find this remark amusing and sullenly shows us to a table near the door so that we have periodic icy blasts as people come and go.

25th November 2003

New York. Staying at the Pierre, one of the best hotels in the city. Checked in and was asked if I wanted a smoking or non-smoking room. I said 'non-smoking' and was shown to an attractive room on one of the top floors. It smelt heavily of cigars, so I went downstairs immediately and confronted the serious young woman in a serious executive suit who I'd spoken to previously. 'I'm afraid the room you've given me is a smoking room. There's a strong smell of cigars.'

'Oh. Let me check.' She punched a number of keys on the computer and read some information from the screen. 'That's not a smoking room,' she said, 'that room is optional.'

'What does that mean?'

'It means you can smoke in it if you want to.'

It took me a few seconds to assimilate this information. 'But surely that means it's a smoking room?'

'No. It's *optional*. You can smoke, if you want to.' Her emphasis on certain words made it clear she thought she was talking to an idiot.

'So, I assume that in a smoking room it is compulsory to smoke. Do you have people who call in and check the occupants really are smoking and not just sitting around watching TV?'

This remark earned me only an icy stare. Then ... 'There are only smoking and *optional* rooms available. If a non-smoking room becomes available tomorrow we'll let you know.'

'Thank you.' I went meekly back to my cigar-fumed optional smoking room.

Coffee with Alfred Uhry, the writer of *Driving Miss Daisy*. We commiserate with each other over our failure to film his other hit play, *The Last Night of Ballyhoo*. It was set up at Disney, who then had a change of mind (they did the same thing with *Daisy*). It then fell into the hands of two women producers who cut the budget from $17 million to $225,000 and wanted me to do it on video. Even I knew this was an insane proposition.

Lunch with Richard Maltby Jnr, writer of *Miss Potter*. This brilliant script has looked like it was going to be made half a dozen times. The producer, Mike Medavoy, is still trying to persuade Renée Zellweger to do it. Could she play a shy English lady in Victorian England? Maybe. I'm constantly amazed at how actors can transform themselves.

Saw Horton Foote,* the writer of *Tender Mercies*. He's now 88 and still writing. His new plays seem to be just as good as the ones he wrote 60 years ago. I recall when the script of TM arrived at my house in Sydney. I was so stunned at the quality of the dialogue and the characters involved that I couldn't even wait to finish it

---

* Horton Foote won the Academy Award for Best Screenplay for *Tender Mercies* (1983) as well as for *To Kill a Mockingbird* (1962). His numerous plays include *The Trip to Bountiful*, *The Roads to Home* and *The Young Man from Atlanta* — for which he won a Pulitzer prize.

before I dived to the phone to call the New York producer to tell him I'd direct the movie.* I was terrified some other director had the script and would call before me. I rate Horton every bit the equal of Tennessee Williams, Alan Ayckbourn, Marcel Pagnol, Eduardo De Filippo, Feydeau, Wilde and Chekhov. All my favourite playwrights, though I should add David Williamson and Shakespeare.

I've read criticisms of Horton's work that say he always writes about the South and about the people he knows. Seems to be an absurd criticism as this is what all the greatest writers do.

26th November 2003

Coffee with John Simon, the celebrated, witty, even feared, critic of film, theatre and music. We first met in Berlin in 1977, when *Don's Party* was showing at the film festival. It was one of the first Australian features to be shown outside the country. The reception was enthusiastic, although the Russian delegation was shocked at the behaviour of the Australians at the party and asked me what a party would be like with 'ordinary Australians'.

---

* I directed the film in 1982. It won two Academy Awards — Best Actor and Best Writing, Screenplay Written Directly for Screen — and was nominated for Best Picture and Best Director.

With John Simon — celebrated film, theatre and music critic.

They refused to believe me when I told them these were ordinary Australians and not the privileged ones they assumed them to be. The modest house in a Sydney suburb that we used as a location seemed very grand to Russians living under Stalin's austere regime.

John and I go along to Tower records and trawl through the racks, digging out the works of neglected, but gifted, composers . . . Guarneri, Hovhaness, Hahn, Finzi, Moeran, and a few others. John tells me he'll have to move from his Manhattan apartment to a house in the suburbs as his wife has claustrophobia and can't travel in the lift and climbing the stairs is exhausting her.

Three large hardback volumes of his film, theatre and music criticism are to be published.* I'm flattered that he asks me to write the introduction to the volume on film.

In the hotel lobby, I run into Michael Blakemore, the Australian-born theatre director. He's here in New York directing a Michael Frayn play. Over a drink he says, 'Of course we [he means directors] are in a position to have lots of affairs as we meet so many women [he means young actresses].' I counter by saying that the meeting many women bit is true, but the 'lots of affairs' claim is fanciful, certainly in my experience. I asked Jessica Tandy, when we were making *Driving Miss Daisy*, if Elia Kazan

---

* *John Simon on Film: Criticism 1982–2001*; *John Simon on Theatre: Criticism 1974–2003*; and *John Simon on Music: Criticism 1979–2005* were all published in 2005.

had tried to seduce her when she was in the original stage production of *A Streetcar Named Desire*. Kazan was notoriously libidinous. Jessica was very disappointed that he never once made a pass at her, but always behaved with propriety.

27th November 2003

Back in London. I talk on the phone to Ken Tuohy, the new line producer on *Boswell*. He tells me the papers aren't ready to sign for the production. January is more likely, he says.

I know now the film will never happen.

30th November 2003

A few days in Cambridge working with Jeffrey Archer on *Walking Off the Map*. A charming, if quite modest house that once belonged to the poet Rupert Brooke. I am shown to a bedroom and told 'Lady Thatcher stays here'. Not at the moment, though. I have it alone.

Jeffrey has restored a Victorian folly in the garden. His work room is upstairs and his wife, Mary, a distinguished scientist, has the ground floor. Her area has a computer, files and numerous reference books, while his has nothing but a desk, a couple of writing pads, some sharpened pencils, photographs of famous cricketers — and an hour glass. We sit together and Jeffrey makes notes as I go through the script giving my ideas for additions and deletions. The hour glass is turned over when we begin, then once more. At the end of the second hour we stop for a cup of tea — then plunge back into the notes.

We meet at nine the next morning. Jeffrey has made alterations from the day before. I read these through, invariably impressed not just by the speed with which he's worked, but the attention to detail.

One night we go to a concert performance, in Cambridge, of Berlioz's *Beatrice and Benedict*. Jeffrey has little interest in classical music but Mary sings in and supports the Cambridge choir.

2nd December 2003

Back in Sydney. Still working on the adaptation of *Richard Mahony*. Sent pages to Oscar Whitbread and Zelda Rosenbaum, the producers in Melbourne.

8th December 2003

Jasmin Prosser phoned. She still insists she has the money for the film about the spy, Popov. She wants me to send script notes. I told her I could do these if we have a financial deal in place. She said she'd talk to my UK agent, Steve Kenis, and arrange this. Certain I'll never hear from her again.*

11th December 2003

To Gatton, in Queensland, with James Vernon and Andrew Lees. A location survey for their script, *Tent Hill Road*, based on an unsolved murder case in a small town. Gatton is now a big town and almost a suburb of Brisbane. It's clear straight away it won't do as a location for events taking place in the late 1800s. We drive around the countryside looking at other small towns. All too modern. There might be something much further away from Brisbane, but we'll need to arrange for someone to take photographs.

The locals still talk about the murder as if it was recent instead of over 100 years ago. The fascination, no doubt, is because three young people were killed (two sisters and a brother) in a town of only 400 people. Oddly, there were at least six plausible suspects, varying from the father of the murderees to an itinerant schoolteacher and a couple of stockmen. There are a number of books about the case, all of them reaching a different conclusion about the identity of the killer, or killers.

---

* I never have.

15th December 2003

Trying to do five pages a day on the *Richard Mahony* script. Unless I work to a schedule the job will never get done. I know I drive my wife crazy by playing classical music at a high volume as I write.

Made notes on Chris Koch's script, *Highways to a War*. He writes too much dialogue and, oddly enough, his film script dialogue is often not as good as that in his novel. I ask him why the Anglo–Asian woman, such a key character in the book, has been dropped from the script. She's sexy, has a love affair with the main character, has some of the most telling scenes, and is the ideal person to explain Asian attitudes. Chris tells me one of the producers 'thought it was a good idea to dispense with her'. She'll have to go back.

Interviewed about directing opera singers. My answers were tedious, I think, because the questions were dreary. From time to time people get hold of me who are doing PhD theses, usually of monumental dullness. I remember one on *The Fringe Dwellers*,* which was full of fanciful, not to say absurd, theories about the film, offering cerebral interpretations of scenes, camera angles and character motivation that bore no relation to my approach to the material. The prose style was an

---

* Film I directed in 1986 with an all Aboriginal cast, headed by Justine Saunders, Kristina Nehm, Ernie Dingo and Bob Maza.

impenetrable jargon, which, Adam tells me, is much admired by academics. More accessible English tends to be rejected as somehow diminishing the work. The one thing that was quite clear was that the writer had not the faintest idea of how films are actually made or knew anything of a creative process.

More *Walking Off the Map* scenes sent to me by Jeffrey Archer. He follows my script suggestions very precisely, though not slavishly. He resists putting in any implication that Mallory had a couple of homosexual affairs, though it seems likely that he did. There are some very odd nude photographs of Mallory floating around.

Dinner with Barry Humphries, Virginia, Cordelia and Trilby* at Icebergs in Bondi — a converted changing shed for swimmers. Good food and phenomenally expensive; paying for views over the water. Barry is endlessly stopped for autographs. Cordelia leaving tomorrow for Christmas in France with Rhoisin, Adam, Benjamin and a few hundred other people. Rhoisin bought a vast and beautiful Chateau in Normandy with five acres of gardens, two ornamental lakes and two huge 11th-century gatehouses for less than the cost of a two-bedroom apartment in a Sydney suburb.

Saw *Goodbye Lenin* — German satire about the fall of communism. Quite funny, quite touching and surprisingly thoughtful. The dedicated Communists would seem to be

---

* My wife and two daughters.

an easy target for satire but there is something affecting about the woman who cannot accept that the regime has collapsed.

20th December 2003

Ross Edwards'* birthday party — full of musicians, including Nigel Westlake and Peter Sculthorpe. Much talk about the perfidy of agents and the inefficiency of distributors, especially the ABC's marketing of classical discs. Sounds just like the film business.

24th December 2003

Sam Neill phones. He's read the script of *The Women in Black* and likes it, though he thinks he might be too suave to play the father. I point out that the role he played in the dingo/baby movie is roughly similar. Even with Sam Neill and Isabella Rossellini, I don't think we can get the finance for the movie. The backers always insist on such BIG stars that a couple of merely respected names just won't do. And they'll invariably be happier with a

---

* Prolific Australian composer, who also wrote the score for *Paradise Road*. Has written five symphonies, a violin concerto, piano concerto, oboe concerto, etc. I find his music highly individual but accessible and melodic.

big star who can't act/wrong age/physically inappropriate than a gifted middle-ranking one who is perfect for the role in question.

I'm impressed Sam read the script and then phoned me. Most actors just deal through their agents and take months to read anything. Talking to them directly is like getting an audience with the Pope. True, I've formed friendships with quite a few actors over the years, but when it comes to casting they're never the ones I think would be ideal for the roles.

26th December 2003

Boxing Day. Everyone went out on a boat to see the start of the Sydney to Hobart yacht race. I stay in and clean up from yesterday's huge Christmas dinner. Afternoon, watch *Fanny*, directed by Marc Allégret in 1932 — part of the Marcel Pagnol trilogy.* Very much a filmed play. (I read somewhere that Pagnol actually said 'cinema should confine itself to photographing theatre'.) Think they didn't cut any dialogue at all, but it's well acted and shows, yet again, that the best basis for a film is a script with well-observed characters and

---

* French playwright (1895–1974). Had his own film studios in Marseilles. Had many successes, apart from the trilogy — notably *La Femme du Boulanger* (1938), *Topaze* (1951) and *Manon des Sources* (1953).

something to say. Pagnol knew the people he was writing about. Arguing over the child, fathered by Marius but adopted by Panisse, César says to Marius — 'You weren't the father, you didn't give life, the child took it from you. The real father is love and love was given by Panisse.' Raimu is superb as César, the father of Marius, though I think Pierre Fresnay is too upper class, too refined, for Marius.

When Fanny is going to marry an old man, someone points out to her mother that he is rich. 'But she has no pockets in her nightgown,' the mother replies. César says to the sailmaker, after Marius has left Marseilles — 'You make sails so the wind can blow away other people's children.'

At night we watch John's* new film, *Head in the Clouds,* on VHS. It's a World War II resistance story and has terrific production values for its $12 million budget. On the other hand, I feel it's a bit similar to other resistance movies, though the high-profile cast will be helpful — Penelope Cruz, Charlize Theron. Hard to tell how the critics will react. I'm wrong every time I make a prediction. I thought *The Piano* and *The English Patient* had fairly absurd plots but both had universal acclaim. What would I know?

---

* John Duigan, my brother-in-law. Director of some outstanding films, including *The Year My Voice Broke* (1987) and *Flirting* (1991).

27th December 2003

Lunch at Barry Humphries' flat in the Rocks. Present were Barry, Lizzie, Oscar and Rupert.* Plus the photographer Lewis Morley and his wife, Pat, a businessman (in pharmaceuticals), Ian, and his girlfriend, and Virginia, Trilby — and me. Morley took the famous photo of Christine Keeler astride a chair. He said that photo was one he snapped at the last moment. When he saw it in the darkroom he rejected all the other poses.

Ian said Rene Rivkin is a scumbag and had his chauffeur's girlfriend murdered because she knew of some of his business dealings. But he also said that Jeffrey Archer had a witness against him (in the prostitute case) murdered. I checked this at home in a biography and found the woman was killed in a car crash. I fail to see how Archer could have been involved, but conspiracy theorists on the web seem capable of believing the totally improbable. Mohammed Fayed accused Prince Philip and the British secret service of being responsible for the death of Lady Di and his son, Dodi. Yet this means believing that the driver would deliberately drive into a post at high speed in the hope of killing someone in the back seat — and not himself!

Spoke to Jeffrey Smart on the phone. Said he's painting better than ever — in his early eighties. Told me that men who masturbated a lot in their youth are less likely to have

---

* Barry's wife and sons.

prostrate problems. I checked this one on the net and found it's correct. Why do our conversations, which start with discussions about painters and operas, degenerate to this kind of thing?

Spoke to Stephen Jenner re raising finance for Chris Koch's *Highways to a War*. He insists he can find $30 million and that regular producers 'go to the wrong sources'. Doubt if he knows what he's talking about.

It Always Rains on Sunday on TV. Robert Hamer film made by Ealing in 1947. A multi-story film set in the East End after the war. Starts very promisingly but peters out as the various strands are rushed to unsatisfactory conclusions, both emotionally (especially the John McCallum/Googie Withers section) and dramatically. A chase of Macallum in a railway yard is ineptly staged, though Bill Collins, who introduced the film, could talk of little else. I know that these people who introduce movies on TV would quickly be out of a job if they told the audience they were about to watch a pile of rubbish, but I suspect, all the same, that Collins genuinely does like all the dreary old movies he raves on and on about.

Hamer was a gifted director (*Kind Hearts and Coronets*, 1949) whose career went down the drain, Sir Michael Balcon* told me years ago, because of a drinking problem.

---

* Balcon (1896–1977) was head of the famous Ealing Studios. He was Chairman of the British Film Institute Production Board when I worked there from 1966 to 1971.

Balcon said no director could make more than six good films in any case. After that, he was either an alcoholic or creatively wrung out and just working in repeat mode. I think he's accurate on this one. Even John Ford and Howard Hawks only made about six really good films, though there are exceptions like Ingmar Bergman, who must've done at least 20. How am I going? Not that I could compare with Bergman ... or Hawks ... or Ford ... or lots of others ... gosh ... Maybe three or four really good films so far — *Breaker Morant, Tender Mercies, Driving Miss Daisy, Black Robe.* (Must confess I also loved *The Getting of Wisdom,* although the critics didn't share my enthusiasm.)

Amazing to me that the dashing John Macallum didn't become a big Hollywood star. I remember asking him once how he'd missed out, as he was popular in England at a time when James Mason and Stewart Granger were making a move to the USA. He said he just got tied up in stage plays and English movies.

28th December 2003

Quiet. Went to see a documentary film, *Spellbound,* about a national spelling bee in the USA. Well done — fascinating cross-section of kids from different parts of the country, different social groups; shows off aspects of America. All of them, even the most disadvantaged, were optimistic about their future. One bright Spanish girl, a finalist, had a father who spoke no English at all. He herded cows in Texas and explained (subtitles) that the cows didn't speak at all so he had no need to learn English.

Heard Alan Bates died. I should've seen him in England a few weeks ago instead of just talking on the phone.

29th December 2003

Nice obits for Alan Bates in the papers and on the radio. That's it. A few acting roles, a few awards, a couple of obituaries and then — forgotten. Trilby, at 17, has never heard of Errol Flynn, Humphrey Bogart, Clark Gable, etc — all those famous stars of just a few years ago. I suppose I shouldn't be surprised.

Evening. Dinner at Evan Williams' — a film critic. A most amiable guy, though I disagree, inevitably, with a lot of his reviews. He ran a 16mm print (didn't know they still made them) of *Chicago*, which must be one of the very best musicals ever made (although I still prefer Astaire's dance sequences, even though they're all in awful films). The choreography and direction are just superb. Also the lighting by the Australian–South African, Dion Beebe.

One guest has four daughters who have given up their careers (one as an international cellist) to follow the teachings of an Indian guru. It was clear this guru lives in luxury while preaching the virtues of sleeping on dirt floors and living the simple life. She (the Guru) even arranged marriages for two of the girls. Amazing how all this nonsense of 'the wisdom of the East' takes in so many people. Are people there less materialistic than us? Are they living on a higher spiritual plane? I very much doubt it. Judging on my visits to India and China, consumerism is rampant.

3rd January 2004

Canadian film on tape — *The Barbarian Invasions*. A very deft piece written and directed by Denys Arcand. Must be his first film in ten years or more. A few false notes in it, but overall a great piece of writing — about a successful son who returns to Quebec because his father is dying. The father is quite a character — an academic who had left his wife, had a string of mistresses, and is now stuck in a ghastly national health hospital with no visitors. The son bribes the staff into giving him a better room and forces old friends to visit. All the relationships are detailed and the script well structured. Very moving. It has the same characters as a much earlier Arcand film, *The Decline of the American Empire* (1986). Arcand is the equal of Bergman, if not so prolific, in creating multi-dimensional characters and placing them in conflict or presenting fascinating dilemmas. Most scriptwriters these days seem to me to be drawing their inspiration — could that be the word — from other movies, not from their observation of life.

Went with Trilby to early morning session of *Return of the King*, third part of *Lord of the Rings*. Still don't think I can follow all this whimsy, but the achievement in making these three massive films must rank as one of the greatest in film history. The choreography of the battles alone makes all previous efforts look amateurish. Critics go on and on about the battle on the ice in Eisenstein's *Alexander Nevsky*.* Whole books have been written about it. In fact, the battle is so poorly choreographed that the opposing forces are photographed coming from the same direction, simply because Eisenstein never stopped to think the audience would be confused if one group didn't come left to right and the others right to left. Astonishing that in this week's *Guardian* a gaggle of international critics rank David Lynch† as the greatest living film director! Lynch is quirky but I think the sheer obscurity of his films has many critics convinced of their profundity. Peter Jackson doesn't even make it into the top 40, that is, he's not on the list. Nor am I, needless to say, but then I didn't make it into Halliwell's cinema directory until I'd directed 15 films and had two Academy Award nominations. Yet he had Icelandic directors listed who had done one movie.

----

* Admittedly made in 1938, but Eisenstein had divisions of the Russian army to work with and the full support of Stalin.

† Director of *Blue Velvet* (1986), *Twin Peaks* (1990–1991), *Mulholland Drive* (2001), and many other films.

With Barry Crocker, Barry Otto and Barry Humphries. I've no recollection
where we were or what we were doing but I wish I could find that tie.

Sam Neill called to say he likes the part of Shostakovich in *Master Class*. I emailed the producers in London with this news. No response yet. Do they have the money for the film? Did Albert Finney respond to the role of Stalin? Doubt if this one will happen. I suggested Ben Kingsley for a role and the producer said he doesn't think Kingsley is much of an actor! He couldn't be wider of the mark.

4th January 2004

A hot Sunday. Spent nearly all day at the beach. Went early in the morning with Barry Humphries, who commented on young girls in various stages of undress on the beach. Quite appalling, he thought. Wantons. Told me he had a girlfriend at university who he didn't see again after she was about 19. Then, when performing in Perth, he had a call from her son to say she was in hospital, dying. Barry visited her — said it was so odd not to see someone for over 50 years then visit them at the very end of their life. A lot of people recognise BH. Not surprisingly, he finds it disconcerting the way they often point at him and comment from a few feet away.

Love Actually, written and directed by Richard Curtis. Quite funny in places and cleverly constructed, though some of the interweaving stories were dull (Liam Neeson and his son) and at least one absurd (the boy who goes to America in search of girls). Some good moments. Hugh

Grant probably has the best comic timing of any actor I've seen, including Cary Grant. He has a distinctive set of mannerisms, but then so did Grant.

Trilby now studying Coleridge at school. Bit of an improvement. Their literary choices up to now have been abysmal. Much of it minor Australian works and potboilers. Why don't high school kids study the great novels we used to read? Hardy, Thackeray, Conrad. I remember reading *Gaspar Ruiz* when I was around 14 and thinking it had to be the most thrilling story ever written. Has our society moved so far away from the world of these authors that their writing is no longer comprehensible to teenagers?

5th January 2004

Read Nicholas Hammond's and Denny Lawrence's revised script of *Cloudland* — set in Brisbane during World War II, and culminating in a big brawl between American and Australian troops. Better than the first draft but doubt if it could ever find the $20 million or so needed for production. It has the same format as *From Here to Eternity* (1953), where a bunch of stories are told about various characters prior to the attack on Pearl Harbor. The preamble, all the various conflicts, have to be very compelling to sustain interest and I'm not sure that *Cloudland* pulls this off; it's not bad at all, but is it going to attract such a relatively large investment?

Call from Jeffrey Archer about *Walking Off the Map*, though no real news. He hasn't heard from Paul Bettany re playing the lead. Wants me to call him (Bettany) if he turns it down. I'll do it, I guess, but don't like having to talk actors into roles. If they're not madly enthusiastic it's a bit depressing as then I have to direct someone whose heart isn't in it. Actors are notoriously bad judges of scripts, in general, and their decisions are made mostly by whim, pressure from their agents, or, most commonly, after offers of vast amounts of money.

6th January 2004

Read a new draft of a script adapted from David Malouf's novel *Conversations at Curlow Creek*. This third version is by the producer Pat Duggan, an American horse-breeder with an obsession for Malouf's work. Regrettably, Pat's version is clumsy. The structure — Australia in 1826 with flashbacks to Ireland a decade before — has defeated him and his invented dialogue is far too abundant and quite without naturalism.

7th January 2004

Meeting with Peter Rose at Showtime re *Fortunes of Richard Mahony* and *The Women in Black*. Both had been recommended to him but he hadn't yet read either. Seemed to indicate he'd put $500,000 into WIB and is interested in the other for a TV mini-series. Surprised me by telling me he 'never reads scripts'. Evidently, he relies on the advice of others. Most peculiar for someone in charge of film investments, though it's a syndrome I've come across in Hollywood. Studio executives (not all of them) claim they don't have time to read and hand the job over to young college graduates, who then prepare 'coverage', which is just a few pages that gives a plot synopsis and an opinion about the audience appeal of the project. It's these people — the young graduates — who are deciding how to invest millions of dollars.

Talked about the idiosyncrasies of marketing. Peter Rose said *Billy Elliot* took off because it opened during a tube strike in London in 2000; lots of people went to the movies and word of mouth spread fast. I told him about my good luck with *Driving Miss Daisy*. Warners had nothing planned for it, hadn't even seen it, when they realised they didn't have a Christmas release after their film *In Country*, with Bruce Willis, unexpectedly failed at the box office late in 1989. Hurriedly, they looked at all the films in which they had some small investment ($2.5 million in DMD), decided *Daisy* was promotable and then turned the publicity machine on full blast, transforming an art-house film into a major hit.

Afternoon. Meeting with Stephen Jenner, Chris Koch, Sue Milliken and Stephen's lawyer/partner re

Chris' script, *Highways to a War*. Stephen had talked about having the $30 million virtually in the bag, but it's clear from the meeting, due to Sue's incisive questions, that he has nothing and little idea of how to get it. He mentioned an Australian company, but didn't name it, which he says might back the film 100%. I'm dubious about that one.

9th January 2004

Lunch with Jennifer Byrne, a journalist with *The Bulletin*, at Doyles, Watsons Bay. She is writing a profile. I suspect a large-scale hatchet job is in the works. She starts off by trying to establish that I am some kind of right-wing madman(?!), or so her peculiar questions lead me to believe. Abandoning this, she switches to the subject of my capped teeth. This goes on and on and I predict will be a major, if massively uninteresting, part of the article. I explain that I've always had terrible teeth and it reached the point of having them capped or removed. I chose capped, though I'm sure the article will attribute my choice to vanity. She then lures me into some tactless remarks about Australian actors (mainly Toni Collette). I'm sure these will be prominently featured, too, though I'm assured they are 'off the record'. Experience tells me such assurances from journalists are meaningless. My own fault, of course. I should have been more guarded. Oddly, she didn't seem to be particularly interested in my films or any of my ideas about film-making.

Jennifer is married to Andrew Denton, the son of Kit Denton, who wrote a well-known book (which I haven't read) about 'Breaker' Morant. I told her that when I was doing the script for the film, the South Australian Film Corporation told me they'd bought Denton's research material but had agreed that the material could remain (!) at his house in the Blue Mountains. If I called him, they said, I could go and read it. I phoned, but Denton wanted to charge $100 an hour (in 1979!) for access. I asked the SAFC about this; they said they'd sort it out, but I heard no more and never did see Denton's material. I had to go to London, at my own expense, and research the Boer War in the archives of the Imperial War Museum. I also chased down a clutch of Boer War eccentrics for information.

Bill Gavin calls about me speaking to Albert Finney re *Master Class*. Finney's agent is keeping me away from him as he doesn't want Albert doing anything other than big Hollywood films. It's only with those fees that the agent will collect anything substantial.

Bill Anderson phones — the Irish–Australian who edited *Breaker Morant*, a number of my other films and a few for Peter Weir, including *The Truman Show*. A natural talent, who edited scenes with flair and a refined understanding of characterisation, though he is not a moviegoer and knows nothing of film history — not all that unusual in the film business. Orson Welles is reputed to have seen very few films. Bill has now been in Hollywood for some years — living a complicated social life with various wives and girlfriends. In Sydney he was always getting into fights in pubs (not all of which he won) and having motorbike accidents. Witty and likable, but explosive — he once punched a producer who wanted to look at some edited footage without my being present — he's now recovering from a throat operation and has been cleaned out financially by doctors. I'll have to send something to help him out.

Watched *28 Days Later*, a horror film about a virus that's killed nearly everyone. Directed by Danny Boyle, whose strength is design and visuals. On the other hand, the script is not well worked out, the relationships are not believable and the ending very weak. Interestingly, there was an alternative ending on the DVD — though it wasn't much better — the only difference being that the main character is alive instead of dead. They must've CGI'd* him out of final scene as I can't believe they shot it twice.

10th January 2004

Call from Jeffrey Archer. Paul Bettany still hasn't read Mallory script. Email from Bill Gavin to say Albert Finney

---

* Computer Generated Image. Responsible now for most of the elaborate effects in films.

is in Barbados, so hasn't seen *Master Class* script. He never will if his agent can help it.

Coffee with Sue Milliken and Aden Young, who is still as handsome as he was when he played the young Frenchman in *Black Robe* in 1991. Not that surprising, as he was only 18 when we shot the film. Sue reminded me that Russell Crowe was the other young actor sent to me on tape when I was in Toronto. I chose Aden Young. Probably the right choice as he was younger (better for the part) and more innocent looking. A shame he's done relatively little with his career since then. Like so many handsome actors, he doesn't want to trade on his good looks so chooses roles where he's grotesque and/or an amputee. Might be personally satisfying but it's not the way to become a movie star, unless the role is written with the skill of *My Left Foot*.*

Dinner with Virginia and Lizzie Spender at lousy new Italian restaurant in Balmain. This suburb has the worst and most expensive restaurants in Sydney. An accordionist made it hard for us to hear one another. Not only was his playing awful, but he sang and kept up a dreary patter of weak jokes. One waitress (American, I think) was staggeringly beautiful; I didn't comment on this to V and L, knowing this kind of remark rarely goes down well. They appeared not to notice the girl's beauty.

---

* Directed by Jim Sheridan (1989). The handsome Daniel Day Lewis won the Best Actor Academy Award playing an incapacitated mute.

12th January 2004

Working on notes for Caravaggio lecture on Wednesday night at Art Gallery of New South Wales — 'The cinematic aspects of Caravaggio'.

13th January 2004

All day meeting with James Vernon and Andrew Lees about their script, *Tent Hill Road*. The writing is clever and the dialogue believable but they've loaded the story up with so many characters and so many fragmented scenes it's almost impossible to follow. I'm trying to convince them it needs simplifying, with less characters done in more detail. Don't know how I went. They left with a pile of notes. I think, too, they're overly influenced by other films. Always a mistake. Just tell your own story and don't worry about what worked or what didn't in some other movie.

Finished (?) notes for Caravaggio talk. Hope it makes sense. I'm no expert on Caravaggio but have seen the exhibition and done quite a lot of research. The moody lighting of his subjects must have startled critics of the period. He was accused of painting large black areas just to save himself the trouble of having to fill them with detail.

Paul Bettany doesn't want to do the Mallory script. No comment made, just 'no'. I suppose anything else is superfluous. They'll now go to Jude Law. In my view he won't do it as he'll be besieged with huge studio offers because of *Cold Mountain* — considered a masterpiece.

14th January 2004

Home. Denny Lawrence and Nicholas Hammond arrive to discuss their *Cloudland* script. Conference call with Greg Coote,* who says he'll try to raise money for it once we've done a final revision. Greg put some money into *Breaker Morant* when he was with Village Roadshow. Not much, but just enough to get us over the hump. Later, he took the script of *Paradise Road* to Fox and persuaded them to invest.

While we were talking someone calmly walked into the ground floor of the house and took Virginia's computer. There were seven people around. No one saw anything and the dogs didn't bark, though they normally go insane if anyone strange appears.

Lunch with Chris Koch and Milton Osborne, mainly talking about Asia. Milton worked in the Australian diplomatic corps and has written many books. Says Whitlam made a big mistake giving independence to New Guinea when he did as they weren't ready. Had hardly any uni graduates to run the country. Now it's a huge mess and the government has to spend millions trying to help them.

---

* An Australian producer now living in Los Angeles.

Also told me the Hezbollah (Palestinians) captured an American agent, skinned him alive, and sent a tape of this to the US State Department.

Evening. Did my Caravaggio lecture at the Art Gallery. I think I bored them. Must've been 2000 people there. So stressful I had lower back pain. Only had it a few times; most notably when I was getting divorced.

Endless emails about *The Women in Black* — now we're in trouble with money from the US as the strong Australian dollar means we need more American dollars than we did originally.

16th January 2004

At André Fleuren's* place at Hardys Bay. Came up by train. Went for long kayak, windy and choppy.

Brought up a pile of DVDs to run in the evenings after a long day paddling around the bay. Watched *Girl With a Pearl Earring*. Film about Vermeer, beautifully shot but slight, anecdotal. New actress Scarlett Johansson cleverly made up to look like the subject of a famous Vermeer painting. There is hardly any dialogue in the movie. I remember that Colin Firth told me the dialogue was so awful the actors just refused to say it. Probably the film is

---

* Cameraman who did second unit on a number of my films and was lighting cameraman on *Evelyn*.

On location in Malaysia for *Paradise Road*. Cameraman Peter James on extreme right, next to me in potentate mode.

better without it, but mute scene after mute scene makes for a peculiar film. Somebody should be saying something.

17th January 2004

Spent most of day at surfing beach. Perfect water temperature and great waves. *Lost in Translation*, much acclaimed Sofia Coppola film with Bill Murray and Scarlett Johansson (again). Well observed study of two Americans in Tokyo, but not the masterpiece the critics say. Bill Murray is so laid back he often communicates nothing. Endless articles rave on about how funny he is. I don't see it. SJ is glamorous in the Hollywood manner. Seems to be moderately talented. With those looks that's all she needs to be. Not sure why the film opened on a long held shot of her bottom.

18th January 2004

Still at André's. I'm surviving, even though he's a vegetarian. And a good advertisement for it. He looks 35 but is in his 50s. Saw Jim Sheridan's film *In America*. Even though it's sentimental and a bit florid in places I prefer it to *Lost in Translation*. The acting is outstanding (Samantha Morton, Paddy Considine and two young

girls) — Sheriden could get a performance out of a rock
— and the observation is so acute. Always the right angle,
too, for the drama. André was in tears at the end. I'm told
Sheridan rewrites endlessly as he goes along so the films
go weeks over schedule. How do some directors manage
this? I needed two days at the end of *Driving Miss Daisy*
for some drive-by shots. I pointed out to Warners that
we had no exterior shots of the car travelling! They
replied that they didn't think they were necessary. Quite
absurd. Finally, Dick Zanuck* decided I could go for
two days with the cameraman (Peter James) and one
assistant plus a car and doubles for Morgan Freeman and
Jessica Tandy. Tricky stuff to shoot as the film was period
(1940s and 50s) so no other cars could ever be seen. I
had a stack of road signs and had to hammer these into
the ground beside old two-lane highways so we could
run Miss Daisy's car past them. Every shot we did (seven
of them) ended up in the finished film.

Long kayak. Came back battling a strong wind and
current. Under the bridge the current was so strong that
I noticed, when I looked at the shore, that I was moving
slowly backwards.

Picked up a book of Hollywood memoirs by Lenore
Coffee,† a screenwriter of the 1920s, 30s and 40s. She was

---

* Richard Zanuck. Eminent Hollywood producer, son of Darryl F. Zanuck.

† Lenore Coffee (1896–1984) wrote dozens of films, mostly soap operas and
melodramas. Best known is probably *The End of the Affair* (1955).

so naïve when she first went to Hollywood that she was amazed to learn, from a friend, that men's penises were not all exactly the same size.

19th January 2004

Lunch with Tony Pierce-Roberts in North Sydney. British cameraman on a lot of films including about seven Merchant Ivory productions. Seems very pleasant and down to earth. He said the MI films don't do him a lot of good as everyone thinks he can only do lavish period pieces. He took on a reputedly terrible horror film, *Underworld*, to set himself on a different path.

Evening. My desk and bookshelves are awash with scripts. I took a car full to the dump but it doesn't seem to have made much difference. I try to keep the ones aside that are more likely (still not very likely) to become movies . . .

So many projects. All fanciful? Will any of them happen?

The Women in Black: Sue Milliken now in London trying to tie up the finance. It seems we'll have to cut the budget quite a bit. Hope this one works, though.

Walking Off the Map: Very ambitious. Walden films aren't interested. Might be hard to find backers. If we go to a major studio and they take it on (unlikely) there'll be major script rewrites and a lot of interference. Still no actors attached, either.

Highways to a War. I think the 'producer', Stephen Jenner, is more enthusiastic than experienced.

The Dead Wait: Script needed an extensive rewrite as it was all subtext and no text. New version arriving. Can they find finance? Possibly ... if the budget is low enough and there is South African money.

Sequel to *Ryan's Daughter*: Sarah Miles, who starred in the original (35 years ago!) must've called me 50 times about it. I hear she's a noted eccentric who drinks her own urine. This seems to be a trade mark of ratbags.

Curlow Creek: The scripts have been disappointing. Producer has now suggested I adapt the novel.

Hotel Pastis: A witty script by Dick Clement and Ian La Frenais★ from the novel by Peter Mayle. Set in Provence — a welcome location after the ice of Quebec, the dust of Nigeria, the tedium of outback Queensland.

Foolproof: A thriller sent to me by Phil Noyce.† Not a bad script but no actress they've offered it to seems interested in the lead role. Without this, nothing.

Miss Potter. The wonderful Richard Maltby script. Since we lost Cate Blanchett it seems to have fizzled out. I feel, too, that the producer, Mike Medavoy, doesn't really

---

★ These two amiable Englishmen and Los Angeles based scriptwriters have collaborated for many years and have a string of successes for film and TV, including *Porridge* (1974–1977), *Likely Lads* (1976), *Lovejoy* (1986–1994), *The Commitments* (1991), *Still Crazy* (1998), and many more.

† Very successful Australian director: *Rabbit-Proof Fence* (2002), *The Quiet American* (2002), *The Bone Collector* (1999), *Patriot Games* (2002), etc.

want me as director. I feel that if they set it up with another actress I'll be edged out.

Fortunes of Richard Mahony: TV should be interested in this one, but no guarantee they will be. Despite its flaws, this is one of the great Australian novels and would make an epic movie.

Boswell for the Defence: They keep saying finance is coming for this, but I no longer believe it.

Cloudland: A problem in sustaining the interest of the audience before the big brawl between American and Australian troops. As budget is quite large this factor will be off-putting to investors.

22nd January 2004

Sarah Miles faxes and wants me to re-read the sequel to *Ryan's Daughter*. I'll have another look. Not much hope of changing my mind. No one — who hasn't seen the original — will have any idea about the characters or how they relate.

A parakeet knocked itself out on the window. Put it in a box to recover. When it seemed OK I tried to take it out, but it bit my finger very, very hard. Took it the vet in Balmain. Found out the birds are strong enough to actually bite through finger bones.

Concert at Sydney Opera House of Ross Edwards' 4th Symphony and a piece by Chris Gordon, plus a John

Adams memorial to the World Trade Center victims. This was accompanied by a dreadful piece of film consisting of nothing but shots of feet. What could this have meant? Music all quite compelling. Edwards is a terrific talent with a distinctive style. Chris Gordon very gifted, too. I know he is a self-taught composer. It seems such a difficult thing to master. I've made huge efforts to learn to read music for my opera directing ventures but still have only a basic understanding.

Interestingly, the review in the *Sydney Morning Herald* managed not to mention the Edwards work (surely a major musical event?) or the Gordon one at all. They just reviewed the John Adams.

5th February 2004

To Art Gallery to collect my $500 lecture fee in books. Wonderful. Picked out a superb catalogue raisonné of Schiele and one on prehistoric art, plus a few bits and pieces. Lunch with Cordelia, who is unhappy that she is photographing low-budget films that are badly directed. I now think she's sorry she didn't take my advice years ago and opt for directing rather than lighting. I told her at that time that she'd wind up shooting for directors who had little idea what they were doing. If you're going to con your way in the film business, directing is the way to do it. Editors, cameramen, designers and so on must know something about their craft, but a director can have no talent at all and the film will still be made around them. The actors will act, the cameraman will shoot, the editor will edit. Directors with nothing to say (which is most of them) just cover the action from a couple of wide angles then do close-ups on all the people speaking. A film will result from this procedure. It won't have individuality or distinction, but it will be a film.

The Bulletin interview with me came out. As I feared, a basically hostile approach under the guise of being sympathetic. Constant references to my capped teeth (and), a clear implication that my career is on the rocks, despite the fact that I've not been out of work for even a day since I went freelance in 1971. Also, a dig at my disastrous *King David* of 1985. Admittedly the film was awful (not as bad as *A Good Man in Africa*, though — she couldn't have known about that one), but *all* directors have made their share of terrible films. Would she interview Bergman and make a special mention of *The Serpent's Egg*, or Ridley Scott and hammer him over *White Squall*, or emphasise *Gangs of New York* in an interview with Martin Scorsese?

Naturally, my comments about Toni Collette's overacting are prominent, though I was assured these were off the record. This is going to cause a bit of a furor as she's so wildly admired. There was even an article in the *Los Angeles Times* calling her one of the greatest actresses of all time.

Calls from LA re directing *Scrooge* for TV in a three-hour version. The script and songs are charming. They even want my old friend John Lithgow, a delightful and funny man, for the lead.

9th February 2004

After negotiating with my agent re *Scrooge* an email arrives informing me they've changed their mind! A bundle of enthusiastic phone calls while it looks as if the network will be producing the show, then silence and a curt email when it's cancelled. Evidently they're worried about a rival *Christmas Carol* being done with Kelsey Grammar.

Dead Wait script has improved. Less philosophy and more drama. Now to see if Sheryl Crown can raise any money.

An angry email from Toni Collette's agent taking me to task for my comments on her acting and asking if I 'wasn't aware she is a national icon?'. Evidently, it's perfectly OK to paint me as a washed-up hack in print, but any criticism of Toni is forbidden.

A couple of radio stations call asking for an interview. They want me to elaborate on my Toni Collette remarks. I decline. I'm in enough trouble now.

Spoke to Yves Rousset-Rouard, the French producer of *Hotel Pastis*, who seems to be on the level. Bit of a change.

Evidently, Icon (Mel Gibson's company) is interested in *The Women in Black*. Sue is sending them the budget and casting suggestions.*

Stayed with friends, Tim and Renate Yates, at Cobbitty at the weekend. Renate gave me a memoir by her father, a distinguished Viennese dentist, about his arrest and transportation to a concentration camp. The brutality on the journey was horrendous. Luckily, he was released after a year, probably through the intervention of his non-Jewish wife who went to Berlin to plead with the Nazi hierarchy. She didn't appear to have made any progress, when suddenly he turned up in London, where the family had taken refuge.

13th February 2004

News from London that British tax fund concessions for films are all but wiped out. Blair government is saving money — I guess they're paying for the war in Iraq. This probably means the end of *The Women in Black* and *The Dead Wait* as far as British finance is concerned.

Sue Milliken has heard Showtime Australia are sending a script assessment of *The Fortunes of Richard Mahony*. This will almost certainly be hostile. In my experience these things usually are, possibly because the assessors feel they're

---

*   They didn't like the project.

only really doing their job if they point out numerous infelicities. The assessments done on *Driving Miss Daisy*, *Tender Mercies*, *Breaker Morant* and *Black Robe*, probably my four best films, were all negative. The one for *Black Robe*, written by an unnamed Canadian academic (one, no doubt, jealous of the literary success of Brian Moore) — and which arrived, curiously, only a couple of weeks before filming began — was so dismissive that it was only with huge effort and endless arguments that I persuaded the producers not to cancel the production — something they seemed quite determined to do despite the financial loss that would be incurred.

Interestingly, *Driving Miss Daisy* and *Tender Mercies* won the Academy Award for Best Screenplay. *Breaker Morant* was nominated in that category and won the Australian award, while *Black Robe* won the Canadian award for Best Script.

Patrick Duggan, the American who has an option on Malouf's novel *Conversations at Curlow Creek*, called and said he'd pay me to write a script, in view of my dislike of the three different versions he's sent me over the past four years. I think I'll try this. The novel has an interesting story — an Irish policeman is sent out to the bush to hang a captured bushranger — another Irishman. They talk about their past lives. There is a lot of action, and a touching love story, so it could be commercial.

I'm reading three autobiographies ... Gabriel Garcia Marquez, Tim Rice and Eugene Delacroix — the latter is the son of Talleyrand, it is believed. Marquez writes superbly — or his translator does — and seems to have total recall of his entire life. Rice is much more trivial and is inclined to quote his own lyrics at length. Not so interesting in an autobiography even if *Evita* and *Jesus Christ, Superstar* have some of the best lyrics ever written to popular music.

Lunch with Carl Davis,* who is in Sydney conducting the Prokofiev score to *Romeo and Juliet* at the Opera House. He's made a career out of writing and conducting scores to silent films, including the five-plus hour version of *Napoleon* (1927) by Abel Gance. He said there was a score written by Honegger,† but he never finished it as he was too busy having an affair with Madame Gance. He (Davis not Honegger) worked on 'Liverpool Oratorio' with Paul McCartney (which is written entirely by Carl by the sound of it), about whom he did not enthuse.

14th February 2004

As I predicted, the assessment on *The Fortunes of Richard Mahony* was so dismissive of the script it's hard to believe Showtime could want to go ahead with the project. If

---

* American born, British based composer and conductor. He has written numerous scores for TV and feature films.

† Arthur Honegger (1892–1955). Swiss composer, and a member of *Les Six*.

they do they would have no faith in the assessor at all; in which case why bother using him/her? I think I can put a line through this one.

Went to *Romeo and Juliet*, the old Nureyev/Fonteyn film with the score conducted live by Carl Davis. The music is much better than the usual ballet score, but the film is poor. Very badly lit and shot. They didn't even bother to reshoot bits where the dancers made a mistake; some shots were out of focus and the zoom moves were bumpy. I hate ballet in any case, but why the long, long death scenes with someone lying on the floor, while the music clearly seems to be demanding some movement?

Fonteyn (at 42) was far too old to play Juliet and her perpetually startled expression is comical. Nureyev was young (23) and handsome, but the pair of them are absurdly mismatched.

Sue Milliken has had a skiing accident and is cutting her holiday (in Colorado) short.

15th February 2004

Sunday. André Fleuren and I go for a long kayak, to Fort Denison and back. I know this is good exercise and it's fun. If I don't keep fit I'll never pass the draconian medicals they put me through for each film. A few years ago it was all much more casual. The doctor would tap me on the chest, say 'You look pretty good', then fill in the forms approving me for the project. I suppose a few too many allegedly fit directors have dropped dead on set. Now it's usually a full day of tests. On *Evelyn* I had the medical three times as the producers kept changing insurance companies and the new one wouldn't accept the examination results from their predecessors. In the third test, an Irish lady doctor put me on a walking machine then went out to lunch with a final reminder — 'If you get off it, I'll know. You just keep walking.' She was gone an hour and a half.

Saw *Jesse James*, directed by Henry King,* on TV. Oddly, I've never seen it before. Colour film made in 1939 and (mostly) very well lit by George Barnes.† The day for night scenes worked perfectly, except in one sequence, something that can't have been easy to do with the slow stocks available at that time. A strangely structured script by Nunnally Johnson‡ — key scenes for motivation appear to be missing and there is very little interplay between the James brothers, played by Tyrone Power and Henry Fonda. Both look like male models; the reason for this, apart from their good looks, is that their clothes are

---

* American director (1886–1982) who directed 117 films. Best ones: *Twelve O'Clock High* (1949) and *The Gunfighter* (1950).

† American cameraman (1892–1953). His best work probably on *Rebecca* (1940) and *Spellbound* (1945). Later shot a lot of undistinguished DeMille films.

‡ American writer and director (1897–1977). Very prolific. Best known script was *The Grapes of Wrath* (1940).

Evzen Kolar, producer of *Bride of the Wind* and, potentially, of *Stealing Shakespeare*.

far too new and clean. Some very good dialogue, mostly written for the minor characters.

Wrote a lengthy answer to the script assessor's comments on *Richard Mahony*, though I know it's a waste of time. I'm very wary of getting involved in this project if the producers want some script other than the one they have. This was the problem with *And Starring Pancho Villa as Himself*. HBO wanted so many script changes that it added up almost to a rejection of Larry Gelbart's script.

Who writes these script assessments? They're never signed. At least not the ones I've been given over the years. In America I know the studios employ ambitious young college graduates, but in Australia I have no idea who they use. Failed writers? Jealous fellow directors? In England it seems to be the case that the various producers are quite willing to do the job themselves, generally a much better arrangement as the director knows that the person he's talking to is the one who holds the views expressed.

18th February 2004

Script arrives via email from Evzen Kolar* — *Stealing Shakespeare* — about the famous Shakespeare forgers

---

* Producer of *Bride of the Wind*, a film I directed about Alma Mahler. US critics slaughtered it, so distribution around the world was minimal.

(Samuel Ireland and his son, William) of the 18th century. Not a bad idea, but like so many scripts it's ineptly developed. It should be much funnier for a start. Evzen tells me he can raise the finance(!?). I'll do detailed notes and email them.

Almost alone in a Broadway theatre, I see a Kevin Costner directed western, *Open Range*, which had excellent reviews. It is well photographed and Costner and Robert Duvall are both very good, but the film is far too long for its slight story. Problem is (I think) largely that no one can tell Costner what to do. Some of the chat scenes between him and Duvall are fine, while others are interminable and seem meaningless. The romance between Costner and Annette Bening, a gifted actress, is rather dull, in addition to which she appears to have ambled in from the 21st century, while both the leading men are convincingly in the 19th. The plotting often seems weak simply because the audience is given too much time to think about it and can pick up flaws. There are at least four endings, which doesn't help, either. I guess Costner thought that if he could make a fortune out of *Dances with Wolves* (released in England in a five-hour version!) then timing and pacing don't matter. DWW hit at a time when romanticising Indians was fashionable — a good deal of luck involved. The Australian cameraman Dean Semler's superb photography wasn't a drawback, either.

20th February 2004

Spent days doing extensive notes on *Stealing Shakespeare*, which is not really worth all the trouble. It has nothing apart from the basic idea; all the detail is weak, the plotting poor, the characterisations not thought through. No irony and no humour, despite all those people who were duped (including the King, James Boswell and David Garrick), and even though the forgers managed to produce a previously unknown Shakespeare play and his autobiography!

New script from Mark Shivas,* *Miss Garnett's Angel* (script by Laura Jones, based on the novel by Salley Vickers). This is well written. I'll get hold of the novel and read that also.

My agent at William Morris Agency, Steve Rabineau phones to say that the project I have with Phil Noyce, *Foolproof*, has found a backer, BUT, they'll only do it if I *don't* direct. Just what I want to hear. I guess this has to happen. Am I getting old? Past it? Harvey Weinstein wouldn't do *An Unfinished Life*, with me directing. The job went to Lasse Hallström, even though he must've lost Harvey a fortune with *The Shipping News*. Lasse is a great director, though. I wonder if Phil will call me . . .? Doubtful. He'll leave it to the agent to convey the bad news.

---

* English producer of innumerable feature and TV films.

A call from Madeleine St John. I'd phoned her a number of times but had no answer and feared the worst as she's on oxygen permanently. She's OK. Told me her 'oxygen count' is 81. I asked if this was good and she replied, 'Yes, most people would be dead with that, but the doctors think it's good for me.' Again, I had to tell her we have no finance for *The Women in Black*.

The Rake's Progress, an old Rex Harrison film, mediocre, on TV. Looked it up on IMDb* website to find the title was changed in America as the distributors feared the public would think it was a film about gardening. I recall *The Admirable Crichton* had a title change as it was believed they'd think that was a naval film!

I've been told we'll have to change *The Women in Black* as everyone will think it's about nuns. I guess that's possible. No reason to assume they're all ladies working in a department store.

22nd February 2004

Found a copy of the novel *Miss Garnett's Angel* in a Paddington bookshop. Balmain has dozens of hair and nail salons, plenty of indifferent but expensive restaurants and only one small bookshop.

Return to Kandahar on TV, an amateurish but powerful

---

* The Internet Movie Database.

film set in Afghanistan, about a young woman trying to get to Kandahar to rescue her sister, who is threatening suicide. All very depressing. It has one of the most bizarre scenes ever put on film — a bunch of cripples, dozens of them, charge (limp) across the desert to where artificial limbs are being dropped by parachute.

Steve Rabineau says he's doing a deal with Michael Ohoven for Paul Pender (who wrote *Evelyn**) to rewrite the script of *Alicia's Book* under my supervision. Ohoven has already had this rewritten three times, but has been unable to get it made as no director will take it on. No wonder. So far none of the scripts have made any sense. It seems he's obliged to make a film with this title as some German investors have already put in funds. Why is it there is often money for films that don't exist? That don't have a script? While others have excellent scripts and the money can't be found.

23rd February 2004

Spent most of the day reading the novel of *Miss Garnett's Angel*. Not bad, but fairly slight. (The script, by Laura Jones, is more interesting.) The reviews on the back cover are hyperbolic, the way most novel reviews tend to

---

*   Shot in Dublin, 2003, with Pierce Brosnan, Julianna Margulies, Aidan Quinn, Stephen Rea and Alan Bates.

Directing Pierce Brosnan in Dublin on the set of *Evelyn*.

be. Oddly, film, theatre and music reviewers seem to be much more balanced than novel reviewers — where just about everything is acclaimed a 'masterpiece'.

Started raining. And the temperature has dropped 20 degrees C.

24th February 2004

Lunch with Peter James who is going off to shoot a film in Toronto (*The Pacifier*, to be directed by Adam Shankman, starring Vin Diesel), his first feature since we shot *Pancho Villa* in Mexico. He said that John O'Neill — an American doctor-cum-would-be-scriptwriter — is in Sydney. I said, 'You should've brought him along to lunch.' Peter recoiled and said he didn't want to. 'Why not,' I said, 'he's your friend.' 'No, he's not,' Peter replied, 'I'm his friend.'

Saw 1940 film of *Pride and Prejudice* on TV. I'd forgotten how much I admired it. Laurence Olivier and Greer Garson handle the witty brittle dialogue perfectly and their romance is very touching even though both appear a few years too old for the roles. The script credited to Aldous Huxley actually closely follows a stage adaptation by Helen K. Jerome. The direction by Robert Z. Leonard is very straightforward, with the camera always seemingly effortlessly in just the right position to capture every nuance of dialogue and emotion. I knew little about Robert Z. Leonard so checked him up on the internet — there are no secrets any more. He lived from 1889 to 1968 and began his directing career in 1913. It ended in 1957. He directed hundreds of films, and I'm fairly sure that none of them, except *Pride and Prejudice*, would be worth viewing today. Amazing that he sprang to life for the one film. Hard to think of another example, though I suppose George Marshall did it with *Destry Rides Again* with James Stewart and Marlene Dietrich.

25th February 2004

Two scripts from William Morris Agency. One, for TV, *A Hundred Days of Darkness*, about the war in Rwanda. A promising subject, but a poorly written script. Very one-sided and corny dialogue scenes, which are far too long and written with no understanding whatever of Africans. The writer's method of conveying information is to have the central character get into a taxi and ask the driver what's going on in Rwanda!

The second, a thriller called *The Contract*. Conventional hit-man stuff, with elaborate action scenes and scant attention paid to characterisation or plotting. In fact, no attention. Turned both down.*

It seems that my agent, Steve Kenis, has more or less done a development deal on *Hotel Pastis*. I should leave for LA and then London around 10th March for a location survey.

---

* So I thought. I directed *The Contract* the following year.

26th February 2004

House of Sand and Fog has had rave reviews all over the world and three Academy Award nominations, but I found it slow, repetitive and unconvincing. Hard to believe that Ben Kingsley has a nomination for his role. He is quite good, I suppose, but the character is thinly written. The plot is tedious — all about a down and out girl being evicted and an Iranian immigrant (Kingsley) buying her house. Interminable scenes in her lawyer's office as she schemes to get the house back. Ho hum.

Mark Shivas now tells me he can't find any finance for *Miss Garnett's Angel* as the BBC is no longer interested. That was quick.

3rd March 2004

Rehearsing with Jack Thompson and the Australian Chamber Orchestra — a follow-up to Haydn's 'Seven Last Words of Christ'. The ACO have commissioned six Australian writers to write, and a composer, George Lentz, to compose, a kind of oratorio. The music isn't exactly hummable but seems to work with the libretto. I'm not sure what my role is, though I may have helped Jack a bit when I spent some time going through the text with him.

Call from James Vernon in LA to say that Miramax like *Tent Hill Road*, but Harvey Weinstein won't finance it if I direct. (This is getting monotonous.) James asked me what this is all about — but I suppose it can be nothing except that Harvey doesn't like my films. It can't be anything personal because I only met him once for a couple of minutes in The Ivy in London. That couldn't have been enough time for him to develop an intense dislike, though I know I can arouse ire fairly quickly.

5th March 2004

Virginia and I went to Russell Crowe's place at Woolloomooloo. A very lavish flat, facing Fort Denison, decorated, rather unexpectedly, in lush Hollywood style. I guess I expected something more idiosyncratic from such a gifted and outspoken personality.

About a dozen people there. Russell showed us a documentary he made about a motorcycling trip he and some friends did a few years ago from central Queensland to Darwin. Very good — an interesting bunch of characters. Russell's wife didn't make an appearance. I asked about this and was told 'she's very shy'.

Gave Russell two scripts, *Tent Hill Road* and *Highways to a War*. He gave me one to read.

6th March 2004

Russell Crowe's script, *The Long Green Shore*, is too long. Set during World War II there are too many characters and not enough story, or, rather, not enough continuity in the story. No scriptwriter is credited. I called Russell who is sending me the novel it's based on.

11th March 2004

En route to France for a location survey. Flying via USA on a ticket sent by French producer of *Hotel Pastis*. Saw two movies on the plane. *The Night We Called it a Day* — a great title but it must be the worst directed Australian film ever (though it's run a close second by *Dirty Deeds*). Based on the real incident where Frank Sinatra was kept prisoner in a Sydney hotel because he insulted an Australian female journalist. He was told he could leave the country when he apologised. He held out for weeks, then did so. Oddly, the film deals only marginally with this situation. It concerns itself mainly with the problems a young Australian concert promoter is having with his girlfriend and his relationship with his gangster father. A peculiar way of dealing with/ avoiding the story. *Raising Victor Vargas* is a very low-budget film set in New York about a Spanish–American family — two young boys, their sister and domineering grandmother. Well observed and acted, presumably based on real people and incidents. The grandmother is a sensational actress. I wonder if she's a professional.

15th March 2004

Los Angeles. Met with Djimon Hounsou, the African actor nominated for the Best Supporting Actor Academy Award for *In America*. Sheryl Crown has arranged this and flown from London for the meeting, though I know she can't afford it. We meet at the Four Seasons Hotel. Djimon is huge and speaks near-perfect English, though his first language is an African one, and his second French. Sheryl is shattered to find out that he hasn't read *The Dead Wait* and seems to know nothing about it; he obviously doesn't regard this as a serious project. I suppose that, with his nomination, the idea of a low-budget film in South Africa isn't all that appealing. Yet the role . . . of a captured African guerrilla leader and his relationship with his white captors . . . is written with insight and compassion.

I am endlessly amazed at actors' responses, or lack of them, to scripts. Why is it that we couldn't find anyone (except Sam Neill, who the producer inexplicably vetoed), that is any 'name' actor, for *Black Robe*? Yet it's probably the best film I've directed. *Driving Miss Daisy* was actually cancelled at one stage because no one wanted to play the role of Miss Daisy's son. At the very last minute we were saved because of a call from Dan Ackroyd offering his services. He wanted to come and audition for me, but I said, 'Don't worry about that, the role is yours.' Dick Zanuck was apprehensive about Ackroyd being miscast, but I pointed out that if we wanted to make the film we'd better accept him as there was literally no one else. (Ackroyd won an Academy Award nomination for his role.) Further, there was the wonderful script by Timberlake Wertenbaker* of *Our Country's Good* (adapted from Tom Keneally's novel *The Playmaker*), which was to be produced by the prestigious Ismail Merchant. Although fully, if modestly, financed, the film never eventuated as we couldn't find any actors at all, despite approaching a number of them in England, America and Australia. Yet . . . when preparing *Double Jeopardy*† from a script not in the same class as all these, I was inundated with famous names wanting to play quite minor roles.‡ Why?

17th March 2004

Los Angeles. Met, at a noisy sidewalk coffee shop, with Evzen Kolar and the two writers of *Stealing Shakespeare*

---

* American playwright and translator. She has won numerous awards and has long been associated with the Royal Court theatre in London.

† With Tommy Lee Jones, Ashley Judd and Bruce Greenwood.

‡ The same thing happened when casting for *The Contract*.

— an Irishman and a glum English girl. Both, especially the English girl, seemed surprised at my suggestion that the basic story was potentially amusing. From forging Shakespeare's signature the father and son team progressed to letters, then his autobiography and then a play. Following their unmasking and a gaol term they realised there was now a market for the *forged* signatures, so they went ahead and forged new ones, claiming these were the *original* Shakespeare forgeries. It is apparent that if the humour of this situation has to be pointed out to the writers then their attempts to inject some mirth would be fruitless.

I suggest to Evzen that the ideal writer for the project — for a new script, not a rewrite — would be the Australian Patrick Edgeworth, who wrote the brilliant (but never filmed) *Boswell for the Defence*. I think this is all going to go nowhere as Evzen has no money to pay him in any event.

Read the novel of *The Long Green Shore* by John Hepworth. Unlike the script Russell Crowe gave me, it's quite short. The descriptions are well done, obviously based on actual experience, but — like the script — there's little characterisation or plot. (I know it's been acclaimed as a masterpiece but this is definitely an overstatement.) It's hard to make war films (maybe any films) work without diverse characters and some conflict between them, in addition to conflict with the enemy. This is what makes movies such as *All Quiet on the Western Front*, *A Walk in the Sun* and *Platoon* so effective. Men look much the same in uniform (as I found out when I directed

Breaker Morant), so unless the characters are distinguishable through physical types and speech patterns the audience can easily confuse them.

19th March 2004

Long meeting with Vincent De Ville and Jim Berry to go through his script of *Semmelweiss* — story of the Hungarian doctor who introduced hygiene into hospitals. The current script has only an effective opening as Semmelweiss is taken to an insane asylum. After that it collapses. Jim shows me a student film, a short, he made about Dr Semmelweiss. Quite an achievement on a low budget, but I point out there is a difference between dramatising an incident in someone's life and making a feature film about them.

25th March 2004

In Provence, looking for locations for *Hotel Pastis*. Have now read the book by Peter Mayle. The script is so different (and much better plotted) than the novel that it surprised me Yves Rousset-Rouard bothered buying the film rights. I suppose Mayle's name is a big draw.

Oddly, I've never been to Provence before. Now is a good time to visit as the weather is fine but the tourist season hasn't begun. Yves Rousset-Rouard and his wife, Marie-Françoise, live in a beautiful cliff-top village, Menerbes, once inhabited by Picasso and Nostradamus, though not at the same time.

Spent about a week driving around the countryside with Marie-Françoise, looking for the ideal village in which to set the story. It must have a square, an inn and a bank. Yves can't be with us as he's fighting a mayoral election.

After seeing dozens of picturesque towns, I finally settle on one, *Oppède*, only a couple of miles from Menerbes.

Despite Yves' charm and enthusiasm I'm not so sure this film is going to happen. Although an experienced producer, who had huge success with the *Emmanuelle* films, he's now more or less retired to the country, where he has a vineyard, is mayor of the town and runs a surprisingly interesting museum of corkscrews. He seems to be out of the film loop. And we're faced with the old problem of attracting a 'name' actor to the project. The script is witty and appealing, but, unfortunately, it's no longer a matter of the script drawing the actor to the project. There are too many other factors, the main one being that the much-in-demand name actors are offered staggering amounts of money for studio films, in addition to which they're attracted by the wide distribution virtually guaranteed those films, no matter how indifferent they might be.

(I remember a lunch with a Hollywood producer who told me he can't get his films cast unless he knows the actor he wants personally and can phone them at home. He said that working through agents and casting directors simply doesn't work as the actors have so many projects being thrust at them they have no time to read them all.)

Also, I've heard a rumour that Ridley Scott is to film another book of Peter Mayle's with a similar (inevitably) story, starring Russell Crowe.* It'll be hard to match that.

28th March 2004

We visit Peter Mayle, a very likable Englishman, now no longer living in the house he made famous in *A Year in Provence*. He said that he was driven mad by the hundreds of Japanese tourists who would stand outside his home waiting for a glimpse of him.

30th March 2004

Marie-Françoise drives me to Marseilles for the flight to London. Yves lost the election. This means he won't be so busy. Should be able to spend more time raising money for the film.

★   *A Good Year* (2006), with Russell Crowe and Abbie Cornish.

Peter Mayle, me and Yves Rousset-Rouard in Provence.

4th April 2004

London. Woke early and went for a walk. On Tottenham Court Road I was looking in a bookshop window when a well-dressed, middle-aged lady came up and pressed a pound coin into my hand. She then said, 'If you go down to the National Gallery, dear, you'll be able to keep warm.' I realised she thought I was a derelict. I was unshaven, but the factor which convinced her, I'm sure, was my fantastically expensive Italian three-quarter length coat. It is artfully distressed, though the end result isn't far removed from the jackets worn by genuine down and outs. Maybe my R.M. Williams moleskins and sneakers added the final touch of decrepitude.

On a play-going binge with Benjamin. *Journeys End* by R.C. Sherriff remains a powerful play about life in the trenches during the First World War. It has no remarkable insights, or even turns of phrase, but impresses just through its sincerity and portrayal of men under stress. Sherriff was an insurance salesman who wrote in his spare time for an amateur company. George Bernard Shaw read the play and recommended its production. It seems no one had much faith in it even then and were all amazed when it was such a success.

Of Mice and Men at the Old Vic. One of the great stories. This production very well played with all the English actors convincingly American not just in their speech patterns, but also their body language.

Baby Doll — the Tennessee Williams play set in the deep South. I remember at the age of 16 thinking the old film with Carroll Baker was so sensual. This production is well designed but the play isn't one of Williams' best and this time the English actors still seem English.

17th April 2004

Back in Australia. Why haven't I been writing this diary regularly? Probably too busy working on various scripts. It takes days to do detailed notes. Often I send these off and hear no more — either they abandon the projects or decide they can't raise the money or decide my notes are worthless and they'd be better off with another director. Whatever the reason, few of those people who send me scripts ever bother to get back in touch if they're not going ahead. A long silence is the only indication I have that either the proposed film is abandoned or that I'm not the director. Once or twice I've found out that I've been replaced by reading it in the paper.

Finished notes on a rambling western story written by the actress Madeleine Stowe and sent to me by Jake Eberts. Don't think there is any potential with this one. A shame, as Jake was behind (financially) both *Driving Miss Daisy* and *Black Robe*. I've sent him a number of scripts since 1991 (*Black Robe*), but he's not been interested in any of them. I've not been enthusiastic about the ones he's sent me . . .

Went to the races at Randwick with Aboriginal friend, Troy Pickwick. His brother was a jockey and Troy sent me an interesting script about the racing game. A tough one to get off the ground — mainly because of expense. I advised Troy to play the Aboriginal card for all it's worth as it might help with funding.

I've never seen a horse race before — only on film. Through Troy's connections we end up in the Members' stand. All the men are in suits and the women — nearly all young and glamorous — are dressed to kill. They all look far more chic than a first night opera audience. No jeans and T-shirts. It's odd to see such a stylish looking bunch tucking into pies and sausage rolls and drinking beer out of cans.

I make a few small bets and lose. Troy wins a few dollars.

18th April 2004

Took Don and Jeanette McAlpine, plus John Stoddart (production designer) to lunch at Doyles, Watsons Bay. It's Don's 70th birthday, though he doesn't look any older to me than he did when I met him in 1971, not long before he photographed *The Adventures of Barry McKenzie*. Since then he's shot ten films for me, including *Breaker Morant*, *Don's Party* and *The Getting of Wisdom*. He turned down both *Tender Mercies* and *Driving Miss Daisy* as the fee was low and his wife didn't like the scripts. (Both films won the Academy Award for Best Screenplay.) A bluff, unpretentious, ex-physical education instructor, he is certainly one of the all-time great lighting cameramen. (His recent work includes *Moulin Rouge, Peter Pan* and *The Chronicles of Narnia*.)

I had forgotten that Jeanette is allergic to seafood. She was gracious about this and said she was happy with just a salad.

20th April 2004

Spent a boring day doing endless notes on a tedious thriller script set in Florida for LA producer, Harel Goldstein. He insists this film is fully financed, though the script is so implausible and so loaded down with stodgy dialogue — and so much of it — that I find this hard to believe. I asked him to send me the novel it's based on and this has turned out to be almost identical. YET ... experience has shown me that scripts being infantile, even amateurish, is not necessarily an impediment to them going into production. It might even be an advantage. So many studio people are happy to commit money to something they've seen many times before, based, I suppose, on the theory that it's likely to work again.

22nd April 2004

My agent calls and tells me that the producers behind *The Contract* want to go ahead with the film and are prepared to do a deal. They know I don't like the script and are happy to have it rewritten either by me or to my instructions. Difficult to resist as other projects don't seem to be moving, or, if they are, it's imperceptible. I have to earn some money and I LIKE to shoot films. Must be careful not to let my enthusiasm for shooting lead me into rash decisions. It did with *Her Alibi* and *A Good Man in Africa*.

24th April 2004

Singapore. I'm invited to the film festival for a special screening of *Black Robe*. Saw a festival film, *Young Adam* — a melodramatic murder/love story set on a barge in Scotland — with Ewan McGregor and directed by David Mackenzie. Takes itself far too seriously. When the third, or fourth, young woman tore her clothes off at the sight of McGregor (who produced the film) the audience started laughing.

25th April 2004

Screening of *Black Robe* a fiasco. I noticed it wasn't in the festival programme and was told this was because the arrangement was made too late. Evidently there was no publicity either, as there were only four young girls in the theatre. None of them spoke English. I sat through the screening. First time I've ever revisited one of my films. Print was good and the sound excellent. I'll always be proud of this one. Sandrine Holt must be one of the most beautiful women ever to appear on screen. She was only 17 when we made the film and oddly, hasn't had much of a subsequent career, though I believe she did a Canadian TV series. Lothaire Bluteau* has had more work, but the fact he speaks English with a French Canadian accent doesn't help.

27th April 2004

Dinner at Oscar Humphries' flat, or a place someone is lending him, in Elizabeth Bay. I felt very old among the collection of astonishingly beautiful young people, all of whom want to be film directors or actors. Oscar and his brother, Rupert, are two of the most handsome men I've ever seen. I've been urging Oscar to take up acting — stardom is inevitable. 'But I have no talent,' he keeps telling me. I assure him this is not a drawback. Reminds me of a line from a Judy Holliday film where she tells some aspiring actor that 'having no talent' can be an advantage, but sometimes 'having no talent is not enough'.

---

* He's done a lot of TV. Apart from *Black Robe*, his main films are *Jesus of Montreal* (1989) and *I Shot Andy Warhol* (1996).

28th April 2004

Go with Barry Humphries to a performance of an Argentinian circus group at Luna Park. They leap around a huge tent, doing astonishing acrobatics with amazing precision far above the ground. 'I could do that,' Barry said.

29th April 2004

A David Williamson play in North Sydney. *Operator* — all about business ethics. Well plotted and well characterised. I don't think I've ever seen a play of his I didn't think was extremely good. I am continually astonished at the range of subject matter — friendships, love affairs, business, law, sports, politics — and the insight, humour and depth with which every topic is handled. How does he research all these things? A shame that they haven't worked too well outside Australia. The few productions I've seen in LA or London were played too broadly, so they appeared to be farces rather than character studies.

3rd May 2004

Met some people from Dendy theatres, with Sue Milliken. They'll invest a modest amount in *The Women in Black*. But will anyone else? Ironic that it's easier for me to set up films outside Australia than here at home.

5th May 2004

In Melbourne. Took part in an ABC panel discussing a play, a film and the Argentinian dancers. Who will watch this? No one, I suspect.

6th May 2004

Paul Pender arrives in Sydney. The colourful Scottish ex-lawyer who wrote *Evelyn*. Now the producer, a handsome German named Michael Ohoven, wants *him* to write a script called *Alicia's Book*. Paul's version will be the fourth. Ohoven doesn't care what it's about, but it can't cost more than $10 million (US) and has to have that title. I suggest he finance *The Women in Black* instead, but this idea is rejected.

13th May 2004

Working every day with Paul Pender. I suggest that the plot can be based around the theft of an antiquity from Thailand (everyone is keen to film in Thailand as it's so cheap). Alicia could be the girlfriend of the thief, or she could be the thief. This could even be vaguely topical as so many countries are now making efforts to prevent the export of artworks.

It's clear to me that Paul's Scottish accent and easygoing manner makes him very attractive to women. As we sit in his hotel lobby, glamorous girls keep coming over, finding an excuse to chat to him, while I am, as usual, invisible. Allure is strange. In Paul's case I think I can understand it, but I have other friends who are magnets to women, though the appeal is not so obvious. Bill Anderson, who edited a number of my films, drew them to him with no discernable effort. I recall once when I was checking in to the Chateau Marmont in Los Angeles and Bill had come to meet me for dinner. As we stood in the lobby, a young woman arrived — also checking in. She took one look at Bill (who is below average height and pleasant looking, but no Adonis) then instantly asked if he was staying in the hotel. He told her he was not. A whispered conversation followed. I retreated to a discreet distance as they made an arrangement to meet later that evening.

15th May 2004

Went to the Great Hall of Sydney University for a performance of a Bruckner mass, conducted by my friend Christopher Bowen. Impressive, but I'm not

Bruckner's biggest fan and find most (not all) masses a bit tedious. I suggest to Chris that they perform Britten's *War Requiem*, which I haven't heard live since 1970. (I went to the Festival Hall in London, with my father who was visiting, and was quite stunned at the sheer beauty of the music and vocal settings. That evening I overheard my father, on the phone to my mother, say of the concert, 'it wasn't much good'.) Chris says the Britten is too complicated. The musical and choral forces are too big for the university choir.

Why is it that I go to so many concerts, operas and plays in Sydney yet *never* run into anyone I knew at university. Where are all those people? Have they left Australia? Are they all dead?

18th May 2004

In Melbourne. I'm invited to be one of the presenters of awards to outstanding high school students. The event is held in an old but restored movie theatre. Most of the recipients of the awards were of Asian origin. 'The new face of Australia,' a professor sitting next to me said. The new face has a work ethic a lot of the old faces would be wise to emulate.

Every speech is prefaced by lugubrious apologies to the 'original owners of this land'. An appropriate sentiment, perhaps, but the repetition seems superfluous.

I go to a smart second-hand bookshop across the road after the ceremony. Find a couple of interesting books on Frank Brangwyn.

20th May 2004

Lunch at the Art Gallery of New South Wales with Barry Pearce, who is writing a book about Jeffrey Smart. Barry wants me to let him have copies of some of Jeffrey's letters to me over the years. I'm hesitant to do this; so much in them is personal and so many comments about people could involve Jeffrey in libel suits.

Liz Gibson, a curator at the Gallery, has lunch with us. She tells me that she taught at a girl's school in North Sydney, where her pupils included Nicole Kidman and Naomi Watts, both of whom talked about how they were going to be movie stars.

A call from London from the producers Ed Pressman and Fred Mueller. (A few years ago I worked for some time with Fred on a project about Kemal Ataturk. We finally had to give it up when we realised that the moment production began we would be assassinated by the Armenians.) They have a project about Rachmaninoff, written by my old friend Tim Prager. Evidently there is a rival Rachmaninoff script, which a Russian company is threatening to make. The suggestion is that I read both scripts, tell which one I prefer (I seem to be under pressure to prefer the one already owned by Pressman and Mueller), after which the Russians are supposed to invest their money into the selected project. All sounds a bit dubious to me. Anyway, I think this Russian script is one that I read some time ago. I had one of my more bizarre conversations about it, in which I was told that 'Rachmaninoff is not known by the younger generation' — the solution to this being that he would never be mentioned by name. Further, he wrote the kind of music young people don't like. This problem would be solved by not using any of his music in the film. 'In what sense,' I asked, 'could this project be construed as being about Rachmaninoff?'

26th May 2004

Lunch at Machiavelli, my favourite restaurant in Australia, with Peter Coleman and Murray Sayle. I first met Peter when I was 17. He was editing a magazine called *Nation*. I charged into his office with an article I'd written complaining about the standard of Australian films, which was published after Peter had forced me to rewrite it a few times. Basically it was an appeal for some Australian feature films presenting our way of life, though my ham-fisted approach didn't endear me to the local producers.

Peter and I have been friends ever since, despite my intellectual inferiority. He has written a number of books, edited *Quadrant* and at one point headed the New South Wales Liberal Party.

Murray Sayle, a dynamic journalist who worked overseas for many years, has now retired to Australia. I've found that many journalists are good listeners. Murray isn't one of them. He dominates the conversation over lunch. Peter and I listen to a long and no doubt acute analysis of the Japanese political system.

1st June 2004

Finished turning the *Richard Mahony* film script into a mini-series. Added 50 pages. Be interesting to see what they think of this. Certainly odd to make a drama which has such a down-beat ending — but that's the story. And the third volume of the novel, the one with Mahony's death, is the best. The description of Mahony's descent into madness, his collapse and death is written with the intensity of Dostoevsky.

Still no movies financed. Lots of phone calls, emails and meetings though.

Read R.C. Sherriff's autobiography, prompted by the excellent production of *Journeys End* in London. Sherriff had quite a career — a number of plays (none as successful as the first), novels, and screenplays — including *Odd Man Out* (1947), one of my favourite films. He's quite frank in the autobiography about his failures and successes but very reticent about his private life. He was devoted to his mother and never once mentions liaisons with women — or men, for that matter. He was a friend of James Whale, who directed the original stage production of *Journeys End* (as well as the film *Bride of Frankenstein* (1935), written by Sherriff) and was a flagrant homosexual — in the 1930s when such leanings were rarely admitted.*

Saw TV mini-series (1994) of *Middlemarch*. Well adapted and very well cast. Must read the novel again.

4th June 2004

Failed again to get Benjamin's Australian passport renewed. He lost it a couple of years ago and renewing it seemed to be a simple matter as all his details are on computer files. But I've been pushed from one Australian consulate to another. From Los Angeles, to Washington, to Sydney, to Canberra, to London, then back to Sydney and now, they insist, London. I point out that the London consulate insisted it could only be renewed in Sydney. Wrong. London.

Delivered *Fortunes of Richard Mahony* in four one-hour episodes. Sue, Zelda and Oscar seem to like it. Not sure where we go from here.

---

* There is an excellent biographical film of Whale's last years, *Gods and Monsters* (1998), directed by Bill Condon.

Saw *The Day After Tomorrow*, which has some terrific computer effects — ice engulfing North America, huge waves down 5th Avenue. Story is unlikely, to put it mildly, with the only scientist who seems to know anything about the weather ambling off across the ice and snow to New York to find his son. Much better, though, than Roland Emmerich's previous films *Godzilla* and *Independence Day*.

James Vernon thinks he has the finance for *Tent Hill Road*. I have a new draft of the script but still can't follow all of the story. In the various revisions he and Andrew Lees have shuffled scenes around but never addressed what I consider to be the problems. There are too many characters, too many short scenes, not enough scenes with the various suspects in the murder, and too little character development of the principals. Overall there is too much striving for 'atmosphere'. When I point out that the plot can't be followed they say, 'What about *Mulholland Drive*?' True, no one could follow that, and it's true it made money, but it was done by cult director David Lynch who can do no wrong. I doubt if the *Mulholland Drive* example can be applied across the board. Is it a good idea going into a film knowing it is confusing and trusting this will be a virtue? I think Andrew and James want to make an art–house film and I want to make a commercial one.

9th June 2004

Trilby's 18th birthday!

Adam is here for a month or so. Characteristically arrived from Boston with no change of clothes, no ski gear (he's going to a wedding in Thredbo) and no wedding present. Just a rucksack full of Latin and Greek books.

Dinner with David Shire, American composer (including *The Taking of Pelham One Two Three* and *Return to Oz*), who is on his way to Adelaide Cabaret Festival. He was once Barbra Streisand's accompanist. Didn't seem to think she was much fun, but very professional and with a great voice. I always thought her songs were overproduced. TOO perfect and therefore not so interesting.

10th June 2004

Fox studios. I meet some of the cast of *The Fringe Dwellers* to record some material for a DVD of the film. Great to see Kristina Nehm, Justine Saunders and Ernie Dingo again. (Sadly, wonderful Bob Maza died a few years ago.) Everybody talking all at once, the track on DVD is going to be chaotic. Seeing it again, I think *The Fringe Dwellers* stands up well. I first bought the novel it's based on in a London market. A battered paperback copy. I called the publisher to ask if I could be put in touch with the writer, Nene Gare, but was told she had died a few years previously. A couple of years after this I was being interviewed on a TV station in Perth and mentioned the book — and the dead author. The phone rang in the studio; it was Nene Gare. Her publisher was misinformed. After this we met and I found out that the moving story of an Aboriginal girl in a fringe community was based on actual events and characters. Nene's husband, Frank, was an administrator with Aboriginal Affairs in Western Australia and they lived for some time among remote communities. Nene had a wonderful ear for turns of phrase, great compassion and a total lack of affectation. The characters all sprang to life for me from the page — always the most appealing aspect of a script. If the dialogue and characters don't work, then there is little prospect of the whole enterprise working. Yet, it's amazing the number of times I've been told, 'Oh, we can fix the dialogue, that's easy.' It's easy only for the gifted, only to those who listen and are interested in people, behaviour, relationships.

18th June 2004

Talking of terrible dialogue.

Spent two days working with J.D. Zeik, who has flown in from New York, and has been brought in to revise the script of *The Contract*. We meet at his hotel near the Quay. He's tall and lean, probably in his late thirties — teaches

writing at a college somewhere outside New York City.
He also plays guitar and sings in a rock group and is a
fanatical long-distance runner.

We go through the existing script, which makes less
and less sense the more closely I examine it. J.D. says he
can do a revision in two days! He told me he writes so fast
he usually has to conceal how quickly he's worked from
the studios. Said 25 pages a day is invariably no problem.
At first I'm worried about this turn of speed, but then
remember how rapidly Horton Foote could write one
superb play after another — and recall David Williamson
telling me he wrote *Don's Party* over a weekend. J.D.
doesn't have many of his scripts actually filmed, but at
least there are a couple. His biggest success has been *Ronin*
with Robert De Niro. He said De Niro went through the
script, reduced the roles of the other characters and took
all of their best lines for himself, regardless of suitability
for his character. This might explain why the role played
by Sean Bean is almost non-existent; he's reduced to little
more than an extra.

I do a bit of checking and find that *Ronin* had a script
'polish' by David Mamet — uncredited. These script
polishes are quite standard in Hollywood. The first question
always asked with any script, no matter how much it's
admired, is 'Who will we get to do the rewrite?' It never
seems to occur to the producers to get the original writer
to make the changes. This has also produced a situation
where screenplay credits are notoriously unreliable. Some

writers have achieved world fame — and riches — on the basis of a reputation for scripts they didn't write.[*]

The Cherry Orchard, directed by Michael Cacoyannis,[†] with Alan Bates and Charlotte Rampling. I don't think it was ever released in Australia. A strange version of the Chekhov play, with a long added section in Paris and masses of the best dialogue deleted and inferior dialogue added. Apart from Alan Bates the casting isn't effective. Charlotte Rampling doesn't convince as a Russian aristocrat. Alan Bates told me about this film when I was doing *Evelyn* with him. Said it had been a lifelong dream of Cacoyannis and he was shattered when it wasn't a success.

While doing my totally boring and I hope beneficial early morning exercises as dictated by my personal trainer, Con Demetriou (a former Mr Australia), I put on John Ford's *Hurricane* (1937). It must be one of the very few Ford films I'd not previously seen. Not especially good, but some impressive stunt work and special effects. Incredible what could be done without CGI. Jon Hall[‡] couldn't act at all, but was handsome and athletic.

---

[*] In fact, the script credit for *The Contract* went to the two original writers, even though almost none of their work survives in the finished film. J.D. Zeik was later replaced by Timothy Prager, who wrote the bulk of the script and added a plot where there was none. Neither he nor Zeik get any screen credit.

[†] A Greek director best known for *Stella* (1955) and *Zorba the Greek* (1964).

[‡] Jon Hall (1915–1979). This was his only major film. He had a career in B pictures ending up with *Beach Girls and the Monster* in 1965.

20th June 2004

Walking the dog in the park I bump into a neighbour. She comments that 'there is a lot to be said for Osama Bin Laden'. I'm a little taken aback, particularly as Bin Laden makes no secret of his mediaeval attitude toward women. My neighbour offers to explain Osama's admirable qualities to me in detail. I decline. Interesting to me how these people find their admirers. A recent book I've read about the Stasi files amazed me with the number of politicians, students and journalists who were on the payroll in the UK. Yet they *must* have known what a repressive regime was in power in East Germany.

24th June 2004

Showtime have been in touch and don't want to proceed with *Fortunes of Richard Mahony*. I predicted this when I read their damning script assessment months ago. I could be wrong, but still think the script is quite good. Zelda and co are sending it off to the BBC and a few other places.

Steve Rabineau tells me that producer Mike Medavoy says Renée Zellweger will sign to do *Miss Potter*. Rabineau doesn't believe she will; thinks her only aim is to prevent another actress getting the role! Sounds a bit mean, but he could be right. He's very cynical but all too often correct.*

A good French film, *Bon Voyage*, written and directed by Jean-Paul Rappeneau. Structured like a Feydeau farce, with all those ingredients of mistaken identity, etc, it's a clever script about the French fleeing to Bordeaux when the Germans take over Paris. Massive indecision follows as the various groups debate whether to join the resistance, flee to England or collaborate with the Germans. Stunning performances from an ensemble cast, which includes Gerard Depardieu and Isabelle Adjani, the latter displaying an unexpected comic gift. The film was a huge flop in France and I'd be very interested to know why. A few French friends I mentioned it to were totally dismissive of it, but imprecise about the reasons.

At the Sydney film festival, saw Antonioni's 1953 *The Lady Without Camellias*, a bitter story of a young girl trying to be a movie star. Technically extraordinary; every dialogue scene was in one shot — invariably a very complex one with lots of camera and actor moves. His early films were so accomplished that it's hard to imagine why it was not until *L'Avventura* (1960) that he achieved world fame. Later, like so many directors, he seemed to run out of story ideas and just became a photographer — usually of pretentious nonsense like *Zabriskie Point*. I remember him being pointed out to me in 1986 on the

---

* He wasn't correct this time.

Spanish steps in Rome. He was old and infirm, with a minder in tow. He looked as if he wouldn't last out the year, though he's still around.

Barry Humphries is back. Went to dinner with him at his son Oscar's place in Elizabeth Bay. The other guests — two very pretty girls and two young men — are all gorgeous. Made me feel like an old wreck, especially as they all treated me with courtesy and listened attentively when I said anything. Barry told me he'd bought a cookbook written by Joseph Conrad's wife, Jessie, and signed by Conrad. Barry is easily the most fanatical collector of books and paintings that I've ever met, and I don't think I've seen a picture of his that I thought was less than superb, though some of the more lewd nudes may be beyond the boundary of tastefulness. I was surprised when Barry told me he'd found the autograph by Takemitsu* that he got for me ten years ago and then lost! He gave it to me tonight, beautifully framed and with a photograph of Takemitsu. Very thoughtful.

28th June 2004

In Shanghai, where I'm to spend a week working with film students who are all attending a course run by a Canadian, André Loiselle. Not sure what I have to do,

* Japanese composer, died 1996.

or what level the students have reached. I'll find out soon enough. A long flight up here from Sydney, though I saw two good films on the plane, from a choice of 60 — *Tais Toi*, a François Viber comedy with some hilarious scenes and good performances from Gerard Depardieu and Jean Reno, though *L'Auberge Espagnol* is more interesting. About a group of students of different nationalities sharing an apartment in Barcelona. All the nationalities portrayed without clichés.

Shanghai is in the middle of a building boom, to put it mildly. Huge amount of traffic. Freeways everywhere. My hotel is on the outskirts of the city. The desk clerk gave me a bunch of photographs on small cards. These show key areas of the city and are shown to taxi drivers to maximise the chance of showing up in the right place.

29th June 2004

I'm given about half a dozen scripts written by the students and have to decide which one we can film, bearing in mind we only have a few days and a limited budget.

Most are either incomprehensible or too ambitious to be filmed and edited in one week. I select a charming one about a foreigner in Shanghai who is put into a new apartment building, where his neighbours are an elderly Chinese couple unhappy at having been moved from their old run-down neighbourhood. They go back there, with the foreigner, and enjoy a convivial lunch, despite the language barrier.

It turns out this script is not written by a student but a youngish Canadian woman named Sabina who has been here for years and speaks fluent Mandarin. She seems to spend all her time on her mobile phone, chattering in Mandarin or French. At least this script is feasible and the students can make the film, even if they didn't write it.

André Loiselle is an amiable and huge man in his thirties given to endless totally pointless jokes. Today we had the scripts copied — at last — and also translated into Mandarin. Tomorrow we cast and check the locations. After that we film.

Had dinner last night with Sue Jett and Paul Elliot★ in a rooftop restaurant owned by an Australian on the Bund (the heart of old Shanghai by the Su-Zhou River). Sue and Paul have been here for six months producing a big-budget American film, *Ultraviolet*, with Milla Jovovich, who Sue described succinctly as 'mad', plus a director they can't stand. It seems he combines arrogance with a lack of technical knowledge. They've finished and leave for home at the end of the week.

★ Sue produced *And Starring Pancho Villa as Himself*. Paul was a cameraman on the second unit.

1st July 2004

The film students are a pleasant bunch (the girls are ALL beautiful); a couple speak perfect English, some a bit of English and some none at all, but it's clear they've had virtually no film training. I think their course is more about graphic design, as they don't seem to have any knowledge of how to block a scene with the actors or how to select angles that will cut together. I'm very much in favour of film schools, though a lot of them are in the grip of film buffs (a notoriously maladjusted species) who have little knowledge of practical filming and less knowledge of the creative process. The best directors make their films from their observations of life, not from the constant viewing of other movies. Bergman has been mining his torrid love life for years, Woody Allen his neuroses, Scorcese his Italian–American roots, etc.

With the help of the multi-lingual Sabina, we miraculously found the two apartment locations and the market we need for the shoot. I encouraged the student selected to direct, a boy named Kaddafi, to storyboard his shots so we'd all know what had to be achieved. He took my advice, but the storyboards turned out to be more fanciful than practical, many of his drawings presenting camera angles that lenses don't encompass. I redid them all myself, then went through them with him. Morale will collapse if we don't succeed in making the film.

With film students in Shanghai.

A film student in non-traditional dress.

2nd July 2004

Somehow Sabina found an elderly couple who agreed to play the main roles — the locals who meet the foreigner. Surprisingly, the old man speaks quite good English. He was an engineer and worked on a number of projects with Americans. We rush from location to location. A modern apartment in a new block (Sabina's apartment, I think), a street market, finally an old tenement building, still packed with residents. We shoot in the one tiny room, having carried the equipment up four flights of stairs. Everyone remains good humoured, though I get the feeling there are no Zhang Yimous or Chen Kaiges among this lot.

3rd July 2004

The end-of-shoot party was held tonight at a Japanese restaurant where they supply all you can eat and drink for about $A10. The drinking was prodigious; sake was being poured into beer mugs and swilled down. André drank five of these. I thought he'd collapse and die. All of the boys drank far too much, the girls were smart enough to avoid more than a sip or two. I detest hangovers and resisted spirited attempts to force one of the sake mugs down my throat.

4th July 2004

This morning, all the boys, especially André, present a miserable sight. They are lying around the hotel, about ten to a darkened room, nursing their headaches. The hilarity of the past three days is no longer in evidence.

Spend the day with Renée Burke, the Irish girl who was the script supervisor on *Evelyn*. She has been working on *Ultraviolet* with Sue Jett and Tony Mark. We go to two big art galleries, one with the best collection of oriental art I've ever seen. A number of paintings from the mediaeval period that are the equal of anything by Rembrandt or Rubens. Evidently nearly all donated by a private collector from Taiwan. Drinks on the 86th floor of the Hilton Hotel — no view because of fog — then we go to a bootleg DVD place, where I am surprised, though I guess I shouldn't be, to see hundreds of copies of *And Starring Pancho Villa as Himself*.

An email to say that Peter Barnes★ died. Awful. A heart attack did him in. He'd married late in life and his wife has just had triplets. He'd called just a couple of weeks ago before he sent me his adaptation of the Noël Coward play *Easy Virtue*.

(By the next morning André has recovered. Cheerful and full of jokes once more. Tells me they'll edit the film and send a DVD of it to me in Sydney.)

★ English playwright, best known for *The Ruling Class*.

6th July 2004

Sydney. David Thwaites calls from Mike Medavoy's office to say Renée Zellweger *is* interested in *Miss Potter* but 'has some thoughts about the script'. Gulp. I've usually found with actresses their 'thoughts' consist of making their part larger while doing all they can to minimise the other roles. I recall going through the script of *Double Jeopardy* with Jodie Foster, who was determined to turn the story into one about a woman's relationship with her father, a plot line that could only be included by eliminating the story we were allegedly filming. After her departure from the project — due to pregnancy — I had to work with her replacement, Michelle Pfeiffer. Similarly obsessive, she was mostly interested in removing the other characters. She even suggested that a key piece of information in a scene could be learnt not from a friend but from a book and dismissed my objection that this would be nowhere near as satisfying for the audience.

David says I'll have to go to Toronto in a couple of weeks to meet with Renée Zellweger.*

Read J.D. Zeik's revised script of *The Contract*. A fast worker, though I'm glad he took more than two days. It's a bit better, though the grandfather has the longest scene in the script. Not a good idea for a minor character. Yet, overall, I feel that the script is not long enough to be a

---

* A meeting that never happened.

feature film (90 minutes). It's typed in a large face, there is a lot of spacing and over-elaborate descriptions of action scenes, which take pages of type but would actually be 30 seconds or less on film.

Randall Emmett calls to say he's talking to John Travolta about *The Contract*. I hope they don't send him the script we have now as he's sure to turn it down.

9th July 2004

Trying to track down some publicity information on *Breaker Morant* for the New York company who are putting out a new DVD. The South Australian Film Corporation, who produced the film, don't seem to have kept any records. They have no publicity material, no posters and no stills. I had a lot of material but gave it all to the Film Archive in Canberra. They 'know they have it' but 'can't find it'. Ended up calling the guys in New York and saying there appears to be nothing whatever to send them for their DVD case. Seems ridiculous.

13th July 2004

More J.D. Zeik revisions arrive. Some improvement, but the dialogue is still perfunctory. All the characters have the same speech patterns, too. When I ask J.D. if the

Washington White House staff would use the same slang and absence of grammar as the tough bad guys he says 'yes'. I very much doubt this. Also, I've found some lines that are lifted from other films. Critics always pick this up so it's inadvisable.

News that Christian Bale loves *Walking Off the Map* and wants to do it.* Dick Zanuck is now giving the script to a Warner's heavy hoping for investment from them.

Saw *Adaptation* on DVD. Quite fascinating, though seems to almost fall apart in the last third. I don't find it believable the New York writer (Meryl Streep) would want to kill the scriptwriter, but is this meant to be fantasy? Tremendous performance from Chris Cooper. I recall that some years ago I saw him on Broadway then tried to persuade various studios in Los Angeles into letting me use him in major roles. They refused. They hadn't heard of him and showed no interest at all. I often wonder how actors ever get their careers started. Must be a large element of luck.

Wrestling with my adaptation of David Malouf's *Conversations at Curlow Creek*. The novel is elegantly written, but has gaps in the narrative that have to be filled in for the film script. I called David and asked about some of the motivation and structure that I didn't understand, but he was quite happy with the ambiguity. In the novel it all seems to work. I suppose the reader supplies the

---

*   This information turned out to be erroneous. The information should have been that he *didn't* want to do it.

unexplained sections from the information supplied. I don't mind ambiguity, but it's something I want to control; there's a difference to me between ambiguity and vagueness. I'd like to *present* possible alternative interpretations of events or character motivation, rather than just leave gaps that are there because I was unsure. Also, I'm bearing in mind something a writer friend, Nicholas Meyer,* said to me recently — 'there is no plot point, however obscure, that can't be explained by a line of dialogue'.

Some years ago when I was asked to do an adaptation of John Le Carré's *The Honourable Schoolboy* I found a number of baffling holes in the plot. I made a list of them and faxed them to the author, with a request for clarification. There was no reply — as I'm sure he had no idea what to say. A lot of acknowledged classics make very little sense at all. Most of Dickens' plots are ridiculous, relying on absurd coincidences and unlikely relationships, but the writing is so vivid and the nasty characters, in particular, so strong that it hardly seems to matter. Others, say, Tolstoy or Jane Austen, present detailed characters and plots that are perfectly logical.

Of course, not everyone reading a novel is expected to break down the construction, event by event, in order to prepare a film script. Certainly, having to *see* the events

---

* Author of a number of novels, including *The Seven-Per-Cent-Solution*, plus many screenplays. He has also directed half a dozen movies.

and characters exposes the plotting relentlessly. Still, I'm constantly surprised at what audiences will accept and reject. Very hard to predict. When I did *Double Jeopardy* a few years ago, I was certain that the storyline would be ridiculed. It was — by the critics — but was a popular film with audiences worldwide.

16th July 2004

Lunch at Margaret Olley's* house in Paddington. A house stuffed full of mementos, including paintings, sculptures, books and dead flowers. If a fire started no one could get out alive. Margaret, although in her eighties and walking with the aid of a Zimmer frame, has cooked lunch for about ten people, all in a kitchen about the size of a phone box; as well as an old stove it has painting materials and a half-finished picture on an easel. I ask the British Ambassador, a guest, what my chances are of getting a British passport as my wife is British, I have a flat in London, worked for the British Film Institute for five years, have been a member of the British Directors Guild since 1969 and two of my children have British passports. 'None whatever,' he tells me. (The passport would come in very handy when I'm asked to direct an EEC financed film.)

---

* The celebrated painter and subject of a famous Dobell portrait.

17th July 2004

I'm given some phone numbers and asked to call Christian Bale about *Walking Off the Map*. The numbers turn out to be wrong.

Pulled a muscle in my leg playing tennis and can hardly walk. Drove out to the sports centre at Homebush and pleaded to be fixed up as I'm going skiing in a couple of days. A very painful massage followed. After that, acupuncture needles were stuck all up and down my leg. I've always been very dubious about this treatment (ever since an assistant of mine ended up in hospital with blood poisoning), but have already noticed a big improvement. I walked away from the treatment centre without doing such a vivid impersonation of a one-legged sailor.

28th July 2004

A week at Mt Hotham skiing with Cordelia. Perfect conditions . . . although there was no ATM. I was told 'we had one, but everyone was using it'. Evidently this was considered to be sufficient justification for getting rid of it. No phones either, other than coin-operated ones. We were meant to fly direct to Mt Hotham but had to land at Albury because of high winds. This meant a tedious four-hour bus trip, with frequent stops to charge us for something or other. When we arrived a passenger called out, 'Arrival charge?'

Cordelia skies very well, far better than me. She can tear down double diamonds that terrify me. Great to spend time with her as she is very bright and can be very witty. Is inclined to go on a bit about her career being in the doldrums, though it seems to me she has plenty of work. I think I similarly always imagine that each job is the last; that everyone will realise I am a fraud and give me no more work.

Watched a couple of the bootleg DVDs I brought back from Shanghai — *I Capture the Castle*, rather quirky and charming, and *The Secret Window*, a cleverly plotted but unsavoury thriller from a Stephen King book.

Heard the Warner's crowd don't like *Walking Off the Map*. Why the hell not? It's an exciting story. A true adventure, the equal of the exploits of Lawrence or Scott. Zanuck is trying some of the other studios. If the studios reject it Zanuck probably won't be able to find finance through the Byzantine independent route with all those complex film boards, minority investors, tax breaks, etc. He doesn't understand that world; it's the new, younger producers, mostly ex-lawyers and agents, who know their way through that labyrinth.

Saw some of *Fanfan La Tulipe*, a remake of the old Gérard Philipe film with Vincent Perez. Easily the best staged swordfighting sequences I've seen, but there are too many of them (!) and an unengaging story with loads of repetition. The film is made with enormous energy but no real wit and no story, rather like *Moulin Rouge*.

Now I hear William Morris Agency are suggesting that Ashley Judd play Beatrix Potter. Plausible? BP was a homely little thing, but then Lawrence of Arabia didn't look anything like Peter O'Toole. Could Ashley do a believable English accent? Anyway, it wouldn't be as absurd as the script she sent me in which she was to play a multiple amputee covered in hair.

30th July 2004

Sheryl Crown is cutting the budget of *The Dead Wait* from $7 million to $3 million. She still won't be able to find the money. It isn't just a matter of a good script, but of all the necessary connections as well as access to a leading actor who will excite the money men. Colin Firth's interest in this project just doesn't seem to be enough as he 'isn't well known in America'.

Lunch with Chris Koch. I told him we are very unlikely to find finance for *Highways to a War*. If I'd had a string of recent hit films it would be much easier! Though the nine Emmy nominations for *Pancho Villa* could help. However, we still have the old problem of trying to find a 'name' actor.

An awful script arrives from Dino De Laurentiis; *The Last Legion* — an inept Roman epic, for which Dino says

he has signed Anthony Hopkins.* Hard to believe that an
actor of Hopkins' stature would take a part in this but I
suppose if the fee is large enough . . . I have such respect
for Dino (who produced *Crimes of the Heart*, which I
made in 1986) and his amazing career (he's been producing
films since 1939) that I'll have to do detailed notes on this
script — which will take me three or four days — even
though I could never see myself directing it. A major part
of Dino's continued success, apart from his financial flair,
is an ability to bounce back from failure. I recall going
with him to the premiere of *Tai-Pan*, a large-scale Oriental
epic starring Bryan Brown. The film was badly received
by the opening night audience and was clearly going to
be a major flop. That night Dino was silent, depressed, but
when I saw him the next morning he was as cheerful as
ever and chatted away with enthusiasm about his future
projects. *Tai-Pan* had already been forgotten.

1st August 2004

Promised Dino I'd read the script again! It won't get
any better.

Read quite a good war script from Harel Goldstein
(*Giant*) with a World War II setting. About a tough

---

* *The Last Legion* has now been filmed, not with Anthony Hopkins, but
Colin Firth and Ben Kingsley.

German soldier who is told to execute a group of crippled children but instead drives them to safety in Switzerland. Final third is implausible and it won't work like this. Harel insists he can find the finance.*

Manon at Opera House. Well sung and good music to a pretty awful libretto. The set and costumes were ridiculous — straight out of 'Dr Who'. Many opera designers and directors around the world seem to have gone quite mad; far more intent on drawing attention to themselves — with productions that ignore the theme and characters of the work allegedly being presented.

I, Robot, directed by the very talented Alex Proyas. Quite stunning computer effects and a well-designed film. Some nice touches in the script (Akiva Goldsman† again), but basically an unsurprising sci-fi plot with the usual elaborately staged and totally unrealistic fights. Movies about plausible human conflict seem to have disappeared. I guess they're there on TV, in various series.

---

* It turned out that Harel is something of a fantasist. He has been unable to finance this film or either of the other two he sent me. Like a lot of aspiring producers, I think he feels that if he tells enough people something is happening then it will.

† My film *Silent Fall* (1994) was the first script of his to be filmed. He's now a top Hollywood scriptwriter. Credits include *The Da Vinci Code* (2006).

7th August 2004

John Travolta isn't interested in *The Contract*. I don't blame him. The script is conventional (though Travolta has done a number of films that were even worse); would've been better to wait until there's an acceptable rewrite. Randall Emmett now tells me they're offering it to Kevin Costner and Bruce Willis(!). If they agree to it I'll be stunned, though with actors, you never know. Emmett says they want to fly me over to LA at the end of this month for meetings.

An email from the *Semmelweiss* producer, Vincent De Ville, to say he wants me to go to Hungary late August for a location survey. He insists that a small LA company will part finance the film, although when I met them some months ago they seemed less than enthusiastic.

Sent notes to Harel Goldstein on *Giant*. How many times have I done detailed notes on scripts — often taking a week to write them out — then have never heard another word.

Still working on *Curlow Creek*. Must've done about 50 pages. God knows what this is like, though it's interesting doing research. Evidently there were army barracks at Wynyard built around 1800 that stretched almost all the way down to the Quay. The biggest barracks ever built in the British Empire. Fascinating, too, to find out the kind of guns the police carried in 1826 and how they fired them. There was a problem, at that time, with

Vincent De Ville: *Semmelweiss* aka *Fever*.

Patrick Duggan: *Curlow Creek*.

bushrangers holding up coaches on Parramatta Road. Hard to imagine now that it's all used car lots.

No news on *Walking Off the Map*. I have a feeling this one isn't going to happen despite the big guns — Jeffrey Archer and Richard Zanuck.

Stephen Jenner keeps emailing saying he has most of the finance for *Highways to a War*. I'm sure he has the Harel Goldstein/Evzen Kolar/Vincent DeVille syndrome — be positive enough, tell enough people it's going to happen and it will. Sue Milliken said she now deletes his emails without reading them.

Peter James is back from shooting in Toronto. His mother is dying of cancer and his father has Alzheimers. Old age can't be much fun.

An excellent *Traviata* at the Opera House. Probably the best opera production I've seen there. Well sung, especially by the Russian soprano — and superbly costumed and lit. Directed with a skill — by Elijah Moshinsky — that brought out every ounce of emotion in the story. Inventively designed by Michael Yeargan.

9th August 2004

Trish* arrives from Baltimore to help sort out all my documents. My study is a mess, dozens of old scripts all

---

* Trish Schweers has been my assistant since 1992.

over the place. We take three carloads of them to the dump and it barely makes any difference.

12th August 2004

Gold Coast. A compilation of clips from my films is one of the opening events at the Film Exhibitors Conference. The clips are OK, but the subsequent interview with the film critic Evan Williams is a failure. I'm not sure if the fault is in Evan's questions or my answers. The audience started talking among themselves, ignoring us on the stage. I don't blame them.

Spent two valuable days with Dale Duguid* having a crash course on CGI effects in films. It's essential to keep up with all the new technical developments otherwise I'll find myself eclipsed even faster by the young hot shots.

Dinner with Herbert Pinter,† who is designing an action film being shot up on the Gold Coast but set in the deep South of the USA. This one evidently features a bunch of popular American wrestlers. There is still no script, though no one seems to be worried about this, I

---

* A computer effects wizard, who did the effects for me in *Paradise Road*, at one point creating an attack by five Japanese Zeroes out of the one plane we filmed.

† Australian production designer who has designed many of my films, including *Pancho Villa*, *Paradise Road*, *Black Robe*, *Bride of the Wind*, *The Fringe Dwellers* and *The Contract*.

guess because it's a genre film for a specialised market —
namely the loonies who follow wrestling on TV, a 'sport'
they must know is completely faked.

Once again I try to persuade Herbert that living in
Fremantle is about the worst place for his career. He won't
move. His wife and kids like it there — in the world's
most isolated city. According to an article I read by the
scientist Tim Flannery, it's going to have to be abandoned
soon anyway as it's running out of water.

16th August 2004

My birthday — dinner tonight with Virginia, Trilby,
Cordelia, Anne Schofield, Trish Schweers, and Peter James.
Sixty-four! I can't believe it. I remember Sir Michael Balcon*
telling me when I worked at the British Film Institute in the
1960s that you never feel any older but just get surprised
when other people regard you as elderly. The occasional
reflection in the mirror isn't too encouraging, either.

Heard from Zelda Rosenbaum that Icon (Mel Gibson's
company) and the BBC also don't like my *Richard Mahony*
script! I still think it's good despite the now almost
universal rejection. Logically, I know I have to be wrong

---

* Head of the famous Ealing Studios (1938–1959). Chairman of the
British Film Institute Production Board (1964–1971). Also the grandfather of
Daniel Day-Lewis.

about this, though just about everyone assured me the scripts of *Tender Mercies* and *Driving Miss Daisy* were worthless. Of course I didn't write those so could have been more objective.

Another draft of *Semmelweiss* arrived today. Steve Rabineau thinks the producers are amateurs, wasting our time. But if they're not serious what are they up to? I'm sure they want to make the film, but without some star attached won't get anywhere approaching the European film funds, which seems to be their plan.

I dive into the revision. It's not much improved despite my detailed notes and laborious discussions some weeks ago in LA with both the producer and writer. Virtually all my suggestions seem to have been ignored. In fact, it's hard to detect the changes. The first 15 pages remain effective and the remainder just collapses into a welter of dull dialogue. The story is so badly told that it's hard to work out what's going on. Yet the basic facts and the various conflicts should be straightforward enough: Dr Semmelweiss was the first doctor — late 19th century — to introduce a policy of hygiene into hospitals. He cut deaths in childbirth from around 30% to nearly nothing, but so upset the medical establishment in Vienna that he was put into an insane asylum and beaten to death.

Call from Randall Emmett to say they're still waiting to hear from Kevin Costner on *The Contract*, but he insists Morgan Freeman is on board. Morgan can't have read the script! He must've been offered a fortune, or maybe is banking on the fact that if we pulled it off with *Driving Miss Daisy* we can do it again.

A call from Isabel Wolff, my 6 foot 4, Irish–American opera agent, to see if I could do a *Manon Lescaut* in Brazil in November! It's possible. She's calling back tomorrow. Will she? She has a habit of phoning me with various opera possibilities then failing to follow up. Directing operas is so interesting — the combination of music and character can produce such intense emotions (in the audience). I'll never forget looking along the row of people at the first night of my 1991 production of *Elektra* in Adelaide and seeing the faces obsessed with the drama on stage. Luckily, that production had a cast that looked plausible. My *Girl of the Golden West* in Spoleto had an overweight, ill-favoured Belgian soprano who couldn't possibly have caused the mayhem among the men of the western community that the story demanded. Unfortunately there are often so few singers who can vocally handle the demanding roles that casting frequently becomes ridiculous. Even Zeferelli's magnificent *Turandot* at the Met had a soprano who looked like a Bulgarian weight-lifter. In fact, she was Bulgarian and will have a second career if her voice gives out.

Spoke to Anthony LaPaglia about *A View from the Bridge*, which he played on Broadway for a year and wants to film. I'll meet him in LA and talk about it. He's a wonderful actor with a strong screen presence but is he a 'bankable' star? I doubt it.

Saw a 1940 British film on TV, *On the Night of the Fire*, which was well reviewed by someone on IMDb but is quite ghastly. Ralph Richardson and Diana Wynyard both far too grand for their working-class roles. Awful cheap sets and incompetent staging, yet so many talented people were involved — the director was Brian Desmond Hurst, the music by Miklos Rosza, and the script from a novel by F.L. Green.

18th August 2004

Re-read the play of *A View from the Bridge* (Arthur Miller). It seems quite dated now and would have to be done as a period piece, but is there any point? Also, it's already been filmed — directed by Sidney Lumet, with the Italian actor Raf Vallone. Plays do date, even quite recent ones. How many of the great hits of the 1920s, 30s, 40s and even 50s and 60s are still performed? Not many. No one does Somerset Maugham plays any more. I find those by Shaw over wordy, polemical and dull. Few of them produced these days. Wilde's plays still work — they're full of insights and not simply amusing.

Meeting with the Film Finance Corporation re *The Women in Black*. Two of the three people Sue Milliken and I met could barely conceal their contempt for the script/project! I could feel their hostility across the room when I first entered. They asked what I most liked about the project. I thought for a moment and said 'the humour'. The female committee member, who could be perfectly cast as a dominatrix in an Almodovar movie, replied, 'But there's no humour in the script.' We're doomed with this lot. A shame as we have part of the finance from England and part from the USA. No point in complaining as the FFC is not under any obligation to finance my pet projects. They have every right to reject. I was so much hoping to call Madeleine St John to tell her we would be making the film.*

Heard a woman being interviewed on ABC radio. She stated that 25% of Australian women are raped. Is this possible? One in four women raped! There are some amazing statistics floating around. While at Mt Hotham, I read a UN report in *The Age* which said that 17% of Australians are illiterate *in any language*. I've not met one illiterate Australian, even when visiting remote Aboriginal communities to cast *Fringe Dwellers* — yet this statistic means nearly *1 in 5* Australians are illiterate. Is it just that I'm mixing in well-educated circles? For that matter, I've not met one Australian who voted for John Howard, but he seems to have no problem in being constantly re-elected. Maybe 17% of Aussies are illiterate.†

---

* Madeleine died in July 2006. I am still trying to find finance for *The Women in Black*.

† Yet according to a website I've checked 99.9% of Australians are *literate*. Could the UN report be so inaccurate?

A visiting Brit production of *Othello*, much acclaimed by local critics. It's in modern dress, which sometimes works, but everyone here rushes around the stage at high speed so their footsteps drown out the dialogue — most of them gabble to such an extent it's incomprehensible anyway. Only the actor playing Othello makes sense of the lines.

19th August 2004

No word from Isabel Wolff about the opera in Brazil. I've called but her assistant has insisted she's out. If the job has fallen through why doesn't she just say so? I don't care. I'd rather know.

The Contract allegedly going ahead. They are confident of finding a second leading man to play alongside Morgan Freeman. Randall Emmett was surprised to hear (from me, during the course of a long phone call) that the seasons are reversed in the southern hemisphere — I told him we couldn't shoot in Romania in January as it would be winter, but not winter in New Zealand, so that's a possible location. He couldn't believe I'd recently been skiing in Australia — it's now so hot in Los Angeles he couldn't believe it's winter somewhere else. Hollywood producers continue to amaze me. Where did they go to school? I remember one who called me when I was editing *Paradise Road* to tell me to change the name 'Singapore' — 'because it's silly'. He was stunned to hear that it's a real city, not a name I invented. Australians shouldn't gloat, though. I recall a dinner party where I told the lady sitting next to me that I'd just come back from making a film in Vienna. 'Oh,' she said, 'that must have been so beautiful. To see all those streets filled with water.' She was so grand that I refrained from pointing out that it was Venice that has the streets filled with water.

Spent all morning recording a 'director's commentary' for the new American DVD of *Breaker Morant*. I hadn't seen the film through since 1980 so it was quite a shock. Oddly, it seemed to be quite good. Amazing how negative so many of the reviews were when it came out. The American distributors were waiting anxiously for the review in *Time* magazine. When it appeared and was dismissive of the film, they lost interest in promoting it. It's resulted in more work for me than any other film I've made, yet was only a moderate critical success and a failure at the box office. It took very little money in America and ran only three days in London where universally hostile reviews killed it.

After lunch (with steadicam operator Simon Harding) I went to Channel 9 to meet with Posie Graeme-Evans re *The Fortunes of Richard Mahony* as a TV mini-series. She is in charge of production. Along with Oscar Whitbread and Zelda Rosenbaum, I'm ushered into an office. We wait a few minutes for Posie, who is a bouncy and self-confident middle-aged lady. Despite her cheerfulness there is an effortless air of authority. When she speaks, or it seems she is about to speak, her assistants fall silent and wait expectantly

In Vienna opera house while filming *Bride of the Wind*.

for the pronouncement. She tells us she quite likes the script (then immediately drags up the old Hollywood chestnut of the rewrite), but is worried about her Channel 9 audience who 'live in Rooty Hill and don't read the SMH'. It always worries me when producers, or any creative people, express such views about audiences. I've never believed they (audiences) were particularly stupid. I've had numerous test screenings in America and have invariably been impressed by many of the comments made by the 'focus group' — usually around 20 people who are chosen at random and then kept after the screening to discuss the film in some detail.

Further, Australian TV stations are producing very little local drama. They prefer those interminable and interminably boring 'reality' shows where the camera eavesdrops on a bunch of masochists being forced to live together. These things cost nothing to produce.

I comment on some rather lurid posters on the wall. It turns out that Posie is also a novelist of some note and these are her most recent works — *The Innocent* and *The Exiled*. I am given a copy of each.

20th August 2004

With a feeling of dread I read one of Posie's books. It is one of the bodice rippers I expected from the posters. I don't want to sound like a snob, although I do, but it seems inconceivable to me that someone who writes this kind of thing is going to respond to *Richard Mahony*. I've usually found that people who write 'popular' fiction, or make low-brow movies, aren't consciously aiming low. They're doing what they like themselves. Those people in Rooty Hill aren't being consulted. They aren't choosing the programmes; they're being fed the kind of stuff that appeals to Posie. Perhaps she's got it right. She's had a huge success with 'MacLeod's Daughters'.

Saw a long German film on DVD, *As Far as My Feet Will Carry Me* (not the catchiest title I've come across), based on a true story about a German POW who escaped from a camp in Siberia and walked to Iran — which took him three years. Some effective scenes but marred by an unlikely relationship with the Russian camp commander — a relationship stolen straight from the fugitive/police chief of *Les Miserables*.

23rd August 2004

Tickets arranged by the *Semmelweiss* producer, Vincent De Ville, for me to go to Hungary on Wednesday. He doesn't have the money for the film but thinks he can raise it in Europe. He must have something if he's paying for my tickets. He's now broken with the LA production company, who wouldn't pay for any pre-production. Or production.

Now Kevin Costner is interested in *The Contract* — I'm told — and wants to meet in LA. He has some 'ideas about the script'. I hope so, as I have none.

Not another word from Isabel Wolff about the opera. She could at least have called and said it's all off — or whatever. Opera agents seem to be a bizarre lot, while film agents are reasonably reliable and sane. My first opera agent was fine — a bright Dutch girl named Eline DeKat, but she quit to join the management of the opera house in Monte Carlo. She was replaced by an irritating gay guy from New York, who never even bothered to come to see my production of *Cold Sassy Tree*★ in Houston. Now I have the immensely tall Isabel who often contacts me about opera projects then goes into limbo.

Watched an excellent thriller (implausible, but this is a defining characteristic of thrillers) *The Bourne Identity* on DVD. Lively direction with terrific stunts (they're *all* so elaborate these days that it must be hard to think of anything new) and good performances from Matt Damon and Chris Cooper. Well-constructed script with a few neat twists. I'm told they did a lot of reshooting and re-cutting. Often happens. At least the end result is good.

2nd September 2004

Flew to Budapest to meet Vincent De Ville re *Semmelweiss*. A long flight. Saw a stack of movies (for the

---

★ Composed by Carlisle Floyd whose operas include *Susannah* and *Of Mice and Men*.

past ten years I've seen more films on planes than in theatres) — *Tom White*, a much acclaimed Australian film with Colin Friels very good in the lead, though the writing is pretentious and the plot unlikely — especially the cliché scene where the derelict (Friels) is picked up and bedded by the beautiful girl. *The Ladykillers* is surprisingly close to the Ealing film original,* though now the action is moved to the deep South. Tom Hanks gives quite a clever performance but the film isn't funny; it's rather cruel, with the gang of crooks nowhere near as sympathetic as the first version. *Man on Fire* is over-directed Tony Scott stuff. Technically well done but with a formulaic story and characters. Also a long documentary about dancers at the Moulin Rouge, many of whom are Australians(!). Interviews revealed a nice but dopey bunch of girls. I found the film depressing despite the many attractive nudes. One of the girls surprised me by remarking that they all much prefer dancing entirely nude as they feel more glamorous and don't have to bother with putting on all those elaborate costumes and headdresses.

Adam's birthday today. He's 33. I still think of him as that little curly headed boy heading off to school. He was (is) so unassuming we initially thought he was a bit dim. Only realised how clever he was when a school headmaster told us he was one of the best students he'd ever encountered.

---

* Made in 1955 with Alec Guinness and Peter Sellers, and directed by Alexander Mackendrick.

3rd September 2004

Budapest is quite spectacular and the group showing me around, all from a local production company, are well organised and pleasant.

The city was destroyed much more during the war than I realised. Many buildings have been rebuilt more or less exactly as they were.

Vincent is convinced he has 60% of the finance for the film, though I'm certain this figure is totally contingent on a batch of factors, certainly on an acceptable cast and a distribution guarantee.

Ghastly massacre in Russia of over 300 people by Chechen rebels. Puts all my petty problems over movies into perspective.

4th September 2004

Location surveys now. Essential to find a large mid-19th century building we can dress up as a hospital. First, a vast ex-military academy closed down by the Russians and now slowly being restored. Could be ideal. The guide told me that after the 1956 uprising the Russians were so furious that they set fire to the National Archives and tore down some buildings they knew the Hungarians adored.

Found a great old house, a mansion, very lavish, though now empty. It was the Chinese embassy until six months ago and has a few strange rooms. One at the top of the house is padded (which makes it totally soundproof) and steel doors have been installed. Who was kept here? Why?

This morning saw a 1940 Hungarian film, *Semmelweis* (the same subject as our proposed film). It was directed by André De Toth, who went to LA that same year and had a long career there (he died in 2002), mostly making B-grade films — including a number of westerns with Randolph Scott.* The film isn't too bad, entirely studio made and very dated with the story romanticised in the 1930s manner. The actor playing Semmelweis was absurd in the early scenes where he was meant to be a student. He was far too old.

I saw De Toth shortly before he died at a tribute night at the Directors Guild in Los Angeles. He was wheeled on stage after the showing of an early, and mediocre, film of his (*None Shall Escape*, 1944) for a Q and A session. At first he didn't seem to know where he was, but slowly became more aware and answered boring questions about his career from the film buff acolyte on stage. (This kind of ending is something I have to avoid at all costs.) I was going to ask him if he agreed with Charles Higham's allegation that Randolph Scott was the lover of Cary Grant, but thought this information might be a bit of a blow to an old man. De Toth has only one eye and yet was selected to direct

---

* *Man in the Saddle* (1951), *Riding Shotgun* (1954) and *Ramrod* (1947).

one of the first 3D movies (*House of Wax*). Strange. Like having a deaf sound recordist or a colourblind designer.

5th September 2004

We visit a vast mid-19th century fort/barracks on the Slovakian border. Probably the biggest single building I've ever seen. It was never attacked — in fact, I couldn't see why invaders wouldn't simply just avoid it. The Russians used it for arms storage. It's now empty but not in bad condition. An English speaking guide — mad, as they so often are; it must be the repetition of information — showed us a corridor 8 km long.

A peculiar lunch in Slovakia with pork and boiled bread. All the small towns are neat and attractive, usually with restored 18th and 19th century houses.

I insist on a visit to Bartók's house in Budapest, now a museum. It was hearing his music (the Second Piano Concerto on the ABC) that first made me aware of the delights of classical music. At the age of 15 I went into a classical record store in Rowe Street, Sydney (the street has now vanished, let alone the shop), and ordered Bartók's String Quartets. They had to be imported. It took months and months. I was so excited when the phone call came to say the discs had arrived. I didn't have enough money to buy them (three LP discs) outright and had to go in and pay them off bit by bit from my pocket money.

Coffee at Gerbaud's, huge coffee shop in the middle of Budapest, with Vincent De Ville and his pretty 20-year-old Hungarian girlfriend who lives in LA and learnt to speak totally fluent Californian English in less than one year.

6th September 2004

Changing planes at Heathrow, en route to LA, I checked my email to find one from Rhoisin telling me that Benjamin has collapsed and is in hospital in Caen, in Normandy. (The nearest hospital to his mother's house near the village of Ecouché.) Evidently he got off the plane from Australia (having left two days before me) and just keeled over. I cancelled the LA flight and flew to Paris, rented a car and drove to Caen. Poor Benji is in bad shape; he has blood clots in his leg and lungs and is wired up to machines and can't be moved. He's cheerful, given the circumstances, but his condition is serious.

7th September 2004

In a city full of beautiful hotels, Rhoisin and I are staying in a ghastly modern place near a motorway as it's close to the hospital. One compensation is that the chef deserves five stars.

10th September 2004

Benji seems a bit better. The hospital is like the one in *Barbarian Invasions* (vast and disorganised), but Rhoisin says it has a good reputation. We call Jane Birkin,[*] who does some checking for us and comes up with an endorsement of the place from top Paris doctors. Benjamin has a photo of his dog, Rosie, by the bed, and his cat, Zeppo, who died a few years ago. Zeppo was a clever cat. He disliked visitors coming to the house and would take their hats and coats and drag them to the front door, where he would place them in a pile, hoping they'd take the hint.

They're letting Benjamin sit up. He only wants to go home, but isn't a difficult patient. He speaks very little French, which makes things a bit awkward, but at least one of the nurses speaks English. In fact, she took her last holidays in Australia.

Had a salad lunch in Caen and found a big slug under the lettuce. They still charged me as I'd 'eaten over half the salad when I found the slug'. They refused to settle for half price.

---

[*] An old friend who has lived in France for many years, where she is a celebrated singer and actress.

Adam is flying over from Boston; he should arrive in a few hours.

12th September 2004

Now Adam is here I feel more relaxed about leaving. Got up at 5 am and drove three hours to Paris. Flew to London, changed planes, then on to LA. Sat next to a fit-looking man who sells family history albums. He asked me if it was true that in Australia the sun rises in the west and sets in the east.

Checked in to Chateau Marmont, after dodging 50 people in the Alamo car rental queue and going upstairs to National where no one was renting at all.

Exhausted.

Called Rhoisin and Benjamin. A scan shows that the clot in his leg is still large and he can't be moved. But he's slowly improving.

17th September 2004

Very busy in LA. Met with Evzen Kolar re his scripts, which will never be done — including the great idea about the Shakespeare signature forgers. Spoke at length with Michael Harrison re the Mario Lanza biopic. Michael, an Australian, has been obsessed with this subject for some years. He moved from Australia to Canada partly because he thought it increased his chances of finding finance. His background is in radio, not film, and it seems to me that he's been meeting up with a lot of fringe enthusiasts who have little chance of getting the film made. From time to time I get a call telling me that investors are poised to finance. Silence invariably follows this pronouncement.

Met with the actor Billy Zane who insists he can sing the Lanza role as well as act it(?!). He offered to take me to a studio where he will demonstrate his prowess. This has to be an example of actor egotism gone wild. I didn't particularly care for Lanza's style, but only Pavarotti has as big a voice. How could Billy Zane coolly make such a claim?

Script from Ken Wales about William Wilberforce. Steve Rabineau says they (Walden Media) 'have money' and want to film 'worthwhile subjects'. Doesn't sound a bad idea. Pretty unusual for Hollywood. The script, by Colin Welland, is surprisingly boring considering that the story is so astonishing. It took Wilberforce over 30 years to push his anti-slavery bills through parliament, and first he had to convince virtually everyone that there was something intrinsically *wrong* with slavery!

Went to Memphis for a day to meet with Morgan Freeman re the lead role in *The Contract*. I stayed in a huge old hotel, the Peabody, in the abandoned (apart from Beale Street) downtown area. Dozens of people gathered in the lobby mid-morning. I joined the group. They were all watching a daily ritual. A group of ducks who ride down in the elevator, waddle across the floor and swim in the fountain.

Morgan and I went to a small coffee shop, still within the hotel, though we'd met outside a stylish-looking restaurant where I'd assumed we would be having a slap-up lunch. Morgan, who hasn't changed since we made *Driving Miss Daisy*, was polite to the numerous people who wanted autographs but asked to be left alone. When an attractive young African–American girl came up to us he was much more chatty. He asked if she was married. She said 'yes'. 'But do you fool around?' he asked.

Morgan is evidently attracted to the script because in it he'll be playing a bad guy. Says he's played so many noble types that people associate him with the roles. He is aware the script needs a lot of work; the only thing he insists on is that he 'doesn't die in the end'. He does at the moment. He points out that audiences won't tolerate it. In another film where he died the audience reaction was so violent the ending had to be reshot. I tell him I'll work out a way to change the ending.

Night. Beale Street is full of jazz clubs, bars and eating houses. All packed. I find a bar stool and order a martini and a stack of ribs. Boring baseball games on the numerous TV sets. The noise is deafening.

Back in LA. Still haven't met Kevin Costner about the other major role in *The Contract*. He wants to meet after a rewrite, so now I have to do MORE notes then try to finalise the script with J.D. Zeik.

Just heard that HBO's party to celebrate their Emmy nominations (including a bunch for *Pancho Villa*) is here in the Chateau Marmont. I'll have to make myself scarce. Couldn't face running into that crowd. They edged me off the film during the final stages of editing. Evidently this happens a lot with HBO films, so I shouldn't feel I've been singled out for bad treatment.

Saw *Collateral*, a well directed if wildly implausible thriller with Tom Cruise and Jamie Foxx. We're asked to accept that a contract killer who has to murder five people will go by taxi, the same taxi, to his killing venues. So well realised and acted (Cruise perfectly cast — his shallowness as an actor works for this contract killer role) that the audience clearly accepted it as realism. Maybe I shouldn't worry so much about the *The Contract*. It certainly isn't less plausible than this. But could I direct it with the flair Michael Mann brings to this film?

18th September 2004

A meeting on the old MGM lot in the Thalberg building. All restored these days (with Japanese money, I'm told) and decorated with hundreds of fascinating posters from mostly forgotten films. There is a project with Jennifer Aniston called *The Diary*. The script is quite amusing and the producers say they would like me to direct, but evidently Miss Aniston is nominating someone she knows. It is clear from the conversation that she will get her way. Star power.

22nd September 2004

Flew to London. Sat next to a young Chinese–American with Tourette syndrome. He kept making involuntary screeching noises. Yet when the hostess, attracted by the racket, came and spoke to him he was perfectly normal. The minute she turned away the screeching began again, then stopped when she turned back. No one adjacent could get any rest.

A few hours sleep in the London apartment then got up at 4.30 am to catch the train to Paris. Subway to Montparnasse and another train to Argentan. Benjamin home now and is greatly improved. He's lost a lot of weight and looks surprisingly healthy.

23rd September 2004

Back to London.

Did extensive notes (again) for J.D. Zeik on *The Contract*. Emailed them off last night. I still fear that J.D. works too fast and is too reliant on old movies for his inspiration. There was actually a scene in his original draft borrowed from *Gunga Din*, of all things.

Spoke to Jeff Smart on the phone. He said a friend of his, in Sydney, told him he'd been very faithful to his wife as he'd only had sex with 14 other women since marrying. In seven years. Two a year. I guess that's not excessive.

4th October 2004

Los Angeles. Read most of Michael Blakemore's* autobiography. Very well done — full of information, and delightfully indiscreet, unlike most 'show biz' memoirs. I wonder if Vanessa Redgrave was thrilled to read the details of her sex life.

Now at Chateau Marmont in vast suite (they all are).

Dinner (expensive) with Vincent De Ville re *Semmelweiss*. He claims to have US$4.2 million of the $6.5 million budget and various people (dubious ones?) are telling him they can find the balance. He's naïve, but enthusiastic. I told him we can't send the script to actors until we have a revision. The current one won't help us. I know I've always campaigned against 'getting a rewrite man, or woman' but with this project it seems essential. Jim Berry's† revisions didn't tackle any of the problems.

---

* Australian theatre director, winner of numerous West End and Broadway awards.

† The original writer.

5th October 2004

Met with Cassian Elwes at last. (He's in charge of a division of William Morris that allegedly finds money for the pet projects of director clients.) He's been elusive for months. I've failed to get an appointment on various trips to Los Angeles, but now I'm in his office confronted by a youthful good-looking man and the inevitable glamorous female assistant. He told me he is trying to find finance for *Miss Potter*. He was surprised the BBC turned it down. Now he has some Miami zillionaire who may be interested. Zillionaires often show interest until their advisors point out to them the immense risks involved — how few films make money, how the distributors are likely to keep it all even if they do. The zillionaires realise they'd be better off sticking their money in a bank — 3% interest is better than nothing at all.

Meeting with Randall Emmett and co in Avi Lerner's office re *The Contract*. There have been dozens of phone calls, but this is the first time I've met Randall. He's very young, probably around 30, very sharp and bouncy, very fast talking. The perfect character to play the lead in a film of Budd Schulberg's, *What Makes Sammy Run?** The meeting was strange. We began with eight people in the room, but one by one they all drifted out, until I was there alone. I waited a while then went into the reception area

---

* A famous 'Hollywood' novel about a go-getting producer.

where the receptionist told me, without any trace of surprise in her voice, that everyone had gone to other meetings around various parts of LA. We hadn't finished *our* meeting, or even started it. I waited a while, realised no one was coming back, then went off to Houle's second-hand bookshop on Beverly.

Before his escape, Randall told me that Morgan Freeman has signed. Provided they get Kevin Costner, Bruce Willis or Nicholas Cage they'll shoot in February. Costner is to get the revised script today . . . it still isn't particularly good. If he has any judgment he'll turn it down, though a big money offer can be very tempting . . .

6th October 2004

More meetings, plus lunch with Larry Gelbart,* who said Robert Redford is driving him mad with a script. He wants endless changes and talks to Larry only through an assistant. Larry, very witty and likeable, tells me his father was a barber in LA. Redford's father was a milkman. I think they are the only two people I've met in LA who were born here.

---

* Writer of the TV series of *M.A.S.H.* (1972–76). Also *Barbarians at the Gate* (1993), *Tootsie* (1982), *And Starring Pancho Villa as Himself* (2003), and many other TV series, movies and plays.

7th October 2004

Cassian Elwes again! Discussed *Miss Potter* financing again! He says he'll try to get an investor with Ashley Judd attached. A shame Cate Blanchett let us down as she was perfect. Also a shame Kate Winslet wasn't interested and that no one but me wants Emily Watson for the eponymous role.

Cassian is supposed to send the *Easy Virtue* script to Diane Lane. She would be perfect for the role of the American woman who marries the younger son of an aristocratic British family.

Lunch with Steve Rabineau. I am not surprised to hear *The Diary* is being directed by someone that Jennifer Aniston wants. *A View from the Bridge* is a possibility — a distant one in my view . . . is Anthony LaPaglia a big enough name for investors? *Semmelweiss* is highly problematic — I think Vincent DeVille is a nice guy but naïve. *Hotel Pastis* is a good comedy project but is probably scuttled because of Ridley Scott's adaptation of a book by the same writer.

I meet a producer* for a drink. He tells me he's been visiting a US$500 per hour Russian hooker who is very beautiful. Said his wife is becoming suspicious of his large cash withdrawals. He is so besotted with her (the Russian girl, certainly not the wife) that he shows me her photo on a website, which displays a variety of gorgeous girls available at fantastic prices. I immediately recognise the girl as a

---

* Litigation or assassination will follow if I reveal this name.

Russian woman who had brought me a script a year or so ago that she wanted to make — all about a Russian woman whose child is adopted by an American couple. I don't let on, but ask him the girl's name. He tells me she goes by the name of Anna, but she told him it's really Natasha. The name the girl gave me was neither of these.

9th October 2004

Visit to Barry Humphries in San Francisco, where he is doing his stage show. The show is screamingly funny even though I've heard most of the jokes before. The audience has a large gay contingent, perhaps not surprising in this city. I go backstage at the end of the show. It always astonishes me how Barry can change from those elaborate Edna Everage outfits into a suit in a couple of minutes. He says goodnight, as courteous as always, to the stage crew and we go to the Mark for a late supper. There is a lounge pianist with whom Barry discusses the more obscure songs of Gershwin, Mercer, etc.

Saw the Brangwyn murals in the Herbst Theatre, a performance space located in the centre of the War Memorial Veterans Building. A small Brangwyn oil of mine is a study for one of them, much to my surprise.*

---

* I've now been told by a Brangwyn expert that my study is by a student of Brangwyn.

The theatre was dark and the managers didn't want to let me in. I pleaded that I'd come all the way from Australia. Finally, some lights were ungraciously turned on and I saw the massive murals. Eight of them, 25 feet high and 12 feet wide, brilliantly colourful and with numerous figures cleverly composed in the vertical format. Each mural shows a season. Two to each. Brangwyn has murals all over America, in various state Parliament houses and in the Rockefeller Center. Yet he never visited America. Just worked from the measurements. He did all the painting at his studio in Ditchling, Surrey.

11th October 2004

Returned to Sydney in a business-class seat in which neither reading light worked. Had to watch movies — awful. *Kill Bill 2* seemed monumentally silly, *The Terminal* is not a bad idea and Tom Hanks is a great actor, but the script doesn't ring true — though it's based on an actual case of a man living in a terminal. The jokey tone is a mistake. *Troy* has some moments, but Brad Pitt is miscast — he seems to be a surfer who ambled on to the set. Dialogue is terrible.

John Howard has won the election, much to the shock/horror of the Intelligentsia. Not to my Greek taxi driver. Someone told me that only taxi drivers vote for John Howard. The country must have a hell of a lot of them.

12th October 2004

Met Sue Milliken and Oscar Whitbread re *Fortunes of Richard Mahony*. Posie, at Channel 9, wants a 'rewrite to make it more commercial'. Problem is, the things she asks for in the notes seem to me to be already there. I've suggested she have it rewritten to her specifications and I'll look at it. Walerian Borowczyk's* *Story of a Sin* on DVD. A film I saw about 25 years ago. (Amazing how many obscure films are available. Does anyone buy or rent them?) Very stylish, luscious visuals, with a narrative that hurtles from one scene to the next with little explanation. The 'extras' on the DVD include an interview with the leading actress — now about 60. She obviously didn't much like Borowczyk, though she thought him talented. A couple of scenes with her were so violent she must've been terrified. She lamented the fact her international career never happened.

13th October 2004

Flew to the Gold Coast to give a talk to a radio group — an association of commercial broadcasters. Seated next to an ex (?) drug addict who told me Thailand is still the

---

* A Polish director, formerly a poster designer, whose career was mainly in France. A remarkable talent, though his later films were obsessed with sexual oddities.

best place for drugs, though Sydney is 'pretty good', and most of western Europe is no problem. He asked me if I'd retired. I must be looking old.

I'm booked to give a talk on 'Celebrity' an hour after Clive James has given a talk on the same subject. Makes things difficult as Clive is witty and an experienced public speaker. It's the same situation as the one where I had to give a short speech at Brian Moore's memorial service in London. I followed Julian Barnes and Seamus Heaney — an eloquent novelist and the best known living poet, respectively.

Clive was as brilliant as I thought he would be. Still, I don't think I did too badly, mainly by being indiscreet about the foibles of some Hollywood celebrities I'd met. I'm a bit anxious that the report in the Gold Coast newspaper could be picked up in Los Angeles. I told the story of how, during a script conference with Jodie Foster, she told me there was no point in disagreeing with her as she was so intelligent she 'couldn't be wrong'. Also told of my visit to Steven Seagal's house, where he was surrounded by a bevy of beautiful Asian girls who bowed and called him 'Master', evidently under the misapprehension, one no doubt implanted by him, that he is the reincarnation of some Tibetan holy man. The producer who drove me to the house confided that Seagal is so out of condition that he's doubled for everything in his films except his close ups. The moment he has to turn and walk away, it's someone else. Needless to say, a group of look–alikes handle all the action scenes.

14th October 2004

This Gold Coast hotel is vast. My suite is as big as my childhood home in Toongabbie and furnished in the Hollywood modern style. There is a vast casino, as garish as anything in Las Vegas, which I suppose is the main attraction of the place. The food in the restaurants, even the breakfast, is almost inedible. Better to walk over to the town for meals. Town is stunningly ugly. Who plans these things? But there are some good restaurants. A group of people who were at the talk ask me to join them. Nice. Friendly. Australians are so amiable; most of them.

Stuck in hotel lift for three-quarters of an hour with six other people. All kept fairly calm. The alarm didn't work, but luckily my mobile did so I could phone the hotel. We finally exited to find the manager waiting for us with a tray of unappetising snacks and a bottle of cheap wine.

Evening. A long long awards presentation — three hours, mostly very tedious. There are more categories in radio than I would have thought possible. The prize giving was broken up with singers and an elaborate pageant with an Australian army band playing an undistinguished piece of music while a soldier read out some sincere but banal poems from soldiers in Gallipoli. It ended with a woman singing a tribute to Aussie soldiers to the tune of 'Auld Lang Syne'. Clive and I found it schmalzy and distasteful, but everyone else thought it very moving. Displays of patriotism always embarrass me.

This was followed by a dinner for at least 1000 people in a huge room. Very noisy. Sat next to a liberal politician, Joe Hockey, who told me he was stunned at the Aussie intellectuals detestation of his party. Labor has been the party of this group for many years, probably since Whitlam was PM. When I was very young the situation was reversed. The Liberals were considered the party of the middle class and intellectuals while Labor represented the 'working man'. When I told Joe I live in Birchgrove he immediately replied, 'Louisa Road! No votes for us there. They all vote for the Greens.' The Greens must have something going for them in their policies as their leader, Bob Brown, isn't going to win any awards for charisma.

16th October 2004

At airport now. Plane has broken down. Two and a half hour delay 'at least'.

20th October 2004

Doing notes on Peter Yeldham's draft of *Drylands* — a script sent about a week ago by my old friend Tony

Buckley.* I don't share all the unqualified admiration for Thea Astley's novel and suspect it was written many years ago. Certainly it doesn't reflect life in Australian country towns as they are now. Maybe in the 1940s. Peter is an accomplished writer, but he has to deal here with an unlikely plot and an unsavoury bunch of main characters. The men, anyway. The women are all saintly. Strange how reviews for mediocre novels are so often just unqualified praise. Critics of film and theatre usually don't hesitate to express a few reservations, or even to be totally hostile. I read an essay some years ago by Evelyn Waugh in which he quoted from enthusiastic reviews of totally forgotten novels, contrasting these with the tepid reviews of his own works.

Still no final news on *The Contract*. My agent insists there is an offer. I'm sure the producers are holding off until another lead is signed.

A phone call from Los Angeles. Pieter Kroonenburg, who I met in London some time ago in connection with a script (by his partner, Julie Allan) about the jazz trumpeter Chet Baker. Now he says he has the finance, provided we can shoot the Californian scenes in Australia. Further he tells me that 'Josh Hartnett definitely wants to do this'. With a star of his stature I can believe that finding the finance wouldn't be all that difficult. I have reservations about the script, but we can deal with that later.

---

* Formerly a gifted film editor and then producer of many films and TV series, including *Caddie* (1976) and *Oyster Farmer* (2004).

Shortly after this a call comes from India. It's my London agent, Steve Kenis, who must be there visiting some client. I mention the Kroonenburg call. Steve is dubious that the finance is really in place.

Sent Joe Hockey two of my films on DVD (*Black Robe* and *Driving Miss Daisy*) along with a letter giving some views on the local industry — mainly a plea for increased government financial support. At the same time, I try to steer clear of the film industry addiction to lauding the virtues of the Labor Party over the Liberals. Politics and talk of politics invariably bores me. I've suffered through so many dinner parties where all the talk is about the perfidy, deviousness and lack of principles of those in government, either in this country or America. Having lived for a couple of years in a seriously corrupt country, Nigeria, I am of the opinion, perhaps a simple-minded one, that the Western democracies are liberal and efficient, overall. A deplorable view according to my friends. Also, I have a strong distaste for dictatorships and have been surprised over the years at the number of those of my acquaintance who have expressed admiration for Castro and even Stalin and Mao. The last two must have killed at least 50 million people between them. This doesn't exactly define their administrations as 'enlightened'. I recall a dinner party where I was accused of being right wing because I voiced some reservations about Castro! I pointed out that he's been in power for 35 years without holding an election, he runs a one party country, controls the press and the trade unions, and gaols homosexuals and political opponents. Maybe they do now have 100% literacy in Cuba, but what is the point if they're not allowed to read anything?

A visit from Michael Borglund, who runs Beyond and who has a commission from the Discovery Channel to do a 90-minute documentary about Australia. Wants to know if I'm interested. It'll all depend on what's happening with *The Contract* or perhaps, hopefully, some other feature.

21st October 2004

Went trawling through piles of DVDs at Rozelle market. I'm always buying copies of my own films, but find it disturbing if they're in the $7 bin rather than the $10 or $15. Often the case, though. I'm always being asked for copies of my films. Everyone assumes that the director is given piles of them, but this isn't the case. My contracts usually stipulate that I'm to be given *one* DVD of the finished movie, though this often proves impossible to actually secure. Found *Evelyn* today. $10.

Chatted for a while to the young man who owns the DVD stall, who tells me he has a boxful of erotic films under the table. I decline to look at them, knowing I didn't direct any of them, but ask who buys them. He surprised me by saying 'mostly young women'. Interesting. I'd have thought the clientele would be old codgers whose sex lives were a distant memory.

I love markets. Amazing what can be found. In London in 1963 I was dead broke. Sifting through a pile of old books on a barrow in a market in Lower Marsh (Waterloo), I came across two books of poetry by Mary Gilmore, both inscribed and signed. I bought them for sixpence each, sent them back to a friend in Sydney who put them into an auction for me. They went for £150, which kept me going for months.

22nd October 2004

Back to Gerard Sutton, eye doctor who's done laser surgery on my eyes twice. He tells me I am unique in having a brain that can't balance the eyes! Still thinks that with another (!) operation he can fix it so I'll have better distance vision and still be able to see my watch without glasses. But will need glasses to read. He now proposes trying various contact lenses to simulate what he wants to do. An alternative is to wait a while and see if my eyes adjust.*

Did interviews for the DVD releases of *The Getting of Wisdom* and *Don's Party*. I couldn't actually watch the films again as all I'd see would be my own inadequacies as a director — so just talked in general terms.

A new Australian opera, *Madeleine Lee* — composed by John Haddock — at the Sydney Opera House. Much acclaimed by the critics but I found it unengaging. A

---

* We waited. They adjusted.

group of American airmen by their crashed plane in the desert are all dead though they don't know it. A search party finds them. Not a bad idea, but the libretto is laborious, the ideas endlessly repeated and the music perfunctory. I must be way out of touch as the audience went wild with enthusiasm at the final curtain.

23rd October 2004

Lunch at Watsons Bay with an old university friend. His love life is complicated. He is having a fling with an old girlfriend, one with a woman he met in a coffee shop, one with a journalist, and (he hopes) one with a redhead he met at the beach. All fantasy? I don't think so.

A good concert at Opera House, included a percussion concerto by Philip Glass, two pieces by Respighi and the *La Strada* suite by Rota. Girl in the lobby had beautiful breasts, almost fully exposed by her black halter top. I suppose girls always know when they have stunning breasts, though know many of them think they have to be huge to be alluring. Quite wrong.

25th October 2004

Lunch with Yves and Marie Françoise Rousset-Rouard at the Quay. They are visiting Australia to see their son who is doing a university course here. Both think they'll still find the money for *Hotel Pastis*. Yves is anxious to have the script rewrite from Ian La Frenais and Dick Clement. Yves has produced a number of films in France, but seems to be out of touch with current financing trends. A charming and handsome couple, middle-aged. Both speak good English. Just as well, as my French is abominable despite 50 years of lessons. I have NO talent for languages, to put it mildly. Once on a cycling holiday with Adam, in Brittany, I spoke to some people in what I thought was passable French, to have Adam say 'you invented three new verbs'.

Did notes on a revised script of *Drylands*. It's improving, but I think it will be difficult to convince anyone this is taking place in Australia in the 21st century.

No word from Randall Emmett re Kevin Costner and *The Contract*.

Call from Chris Koch, who is moving back to Tasmania as living on the mainland is too expensive. He has yet another meeting with Stephen Jenner re *Highways to a War*. How many times now has Stephen told us he has the money for the film? Crazy. Why do producers *manqué* do this? They are invariably so extreme, claiming they have financing of millions of dollars when the most cursory investigation shows they rarely have anything at all. I must be dealing currently with six 'producers' who keep telling me they have finance.

Sent a donation to the Australian Chamber Orchestra. A wonderful group of musicians. Must be a disadvantage being based in Australia when planning tours. So expensive. In Europe all the countries are so close. Even fares across the Atlantic are a fraction of those from Australia to anywhere — except New Zealand.

Dinner with Len Amadio and Bill Gillespie.* Much talk about music and opera, they both thought *Madeleine Lee* much better than I did. I knew Len in Adelaide in the late 1970s — when I was filming *Breaker Morant*. I was fascinated by his habit of falling asleep at dinner parties for 10–15 minutes, then waking and casually rejoining the conversation. He was a bigwig in the Arts programmes in Adelaide when Don Dunstan was Premier. The first time I met Dunstan, Len took me to a Turkish bath where Dunstan was sitting, nude, among a group of young boys. Len and I were nude, too — all a bit awkward.

28th October 2004

Another call from Randall Emmett, now saying he probably wants me to go to LA this weekend to meet with Kevin Costner. Randall is definitely the kind of producer who gets films made. He has all the contacts, knows who to talk to, knows how to structure deals.

---

* Bill Gillespie manages the ACO. An American, now with Australian citizenship, he ran the South Australian Opera Company for many years.

A shame he never reads scripts, so there is no point in trying to impress him with the quality of something. He deals only in terms of 'packages' — the actors and the director.

Saw Tim Wellburn.* He's still out of work. Says they don't even answer his calls and emails. He's an excellent editor. Must be the age thing. He's over 60. So am I. This sent me to a film reference book where a quick search tells me that very few directors work past the age of 55. Almost none past 60. I think most of them just have nothing more to say, others get stuck in a groove (Hitchcock, John Ford) so their films look increasingly old-fashioned as they make essentially the same movie over and over. I think, too, that many become so successful they live sheltered lives, mixing only with the wealthy, so they lose touch with their source material. A friend told me recently he was working with a (fairly young) director who would travel only on a private jet 'accompanied by his personal physician'. An Australian director, working in Canada, issued instructions that anyone who *looked at him* was to be fired. I think I'm free of extreme eccentricities and, I think, have only lost my temper twice on a film set. Once with a script supervisor while shooting *The Club* in Melbourne — she kept insisting the shots we were filming would not cut together (she was wrong, but even a screening of the material didn't stop her complaints); and once with the actor (very talented,

---

* Film editor. Among my films he edited are *Black Robe* and *Paradise Road*.

very miserable and now deceased, happily) J. T. Walsh, after an insane request that he could not simply open the door of a film set to enter the room, but had to go out to the car park, get out of a car, then wend his way through various sound stages until he finally reached the room where we were shooting.

Concert at the Opera House. Mahler's 10th and Berg's violin concerto. Was about to buy a ticket when an obviously well-heeled lady gave me one, saying her friends hadn't shown up. This is the second time I've been lucky with tickets — the first was in 1963 when I was in a queue for Olivier's *Othello*. I'd hoped to be able to buy standing room — all I could afford — when an American tourist came up to me and handed me a ticket for the third row of the front stalls. After all that, I thought Olivier overplayed grotesquely but that Frank Finlay was an effective Iago.

An emotion drenched evening. Mahler has to be heard in a concert hall. Even the best hi-fi doesn't capture the impact or the nuances of the music. The Berg concerto was written in memory of Mahler's daughter, Manon, who died at the age of 18. Intense, moving. I think Berg never heard it; it was not performed until after his death.

31st October 2004

Read five scripts that have been hanging around. All awful.

A Chieftains concert in a run-down old movie theatre in Enmore. Concert was very impressive, especially considering my resistance to Irish folk music. Went backstage afterwards and talked to Paddy Moloney, head of the group, as Pat Duggan had told me he was interested in writing the music for *Curlow Creek*. Moloney had no recollection of the script or of Duggan (who must've exaggerated their acquaintance), but was very polite. Said he had a bleeding ulcer, but was doing another concert in Sydney, then two in Melbourne, then the Gold Coast, Brisbane and Auckland, then on to the Hollywood Bowl.

Spoke to Humphries, who is in Toronto rehearsing his stage show for New York. He's putting in more local references as he's been told the show lacks 'edge', whatever that means.

Read *Hemispheres*, an elaborate but pretentious script aboutsomeCanadiandoctors—thereareincomprehensible/ meaningless links with Australian Aborigines.

2nd November 2004

Tony Buckley has my notes on Peter Yeldham's adaptation of *Drylands*. I hope I wasn't too blunt. Especially as I think Yeldham is a good writer, it's just that the basic story line is unconvincing. On the other hand I could be wrong. The novel has had immense acclaim from literary critics.

Buckley is one of the most decent people I've met in the film industry. Calm, sane, courteous. (How did someone with these attributes become so eminent?) And with an enviable mass of thick hair. He started as a film editor and had a magic touch. He could make even poorly directed films look good and a well-directed one, like *Wake in Fright,*⋆ quite superb.

An email from Randall Emmett to say we'll have a conference call on Thursday morning. I hate these things. They put technology back to the days of Alexander Graham Bell. There are whistles, buzzes, drop outs and usually half the people speaking are so faint they can't be heard.

Lunch with Chris Koch and a friend of his, Warren Reed, who used to be in the overseas branch of ASIO. He said that the failure to find Bin Laden is basically the fault of the British secret service as they're the ones with, traditionally, all the Middle East connections. I told him about the Americans I met in Cannes who assured me that 'everyone in Europe' knows that OBL was a business partner of George Bush and will never be found as Bush is concealing his whereabouts. Reed regarded this piece of information as implausible.

Saw a T-shirt in a store window in Pitt Street with CIA in large letters, and, underneath 'clitoral investigation

---

⋆   Also known as *Outback*, directed by Ted Kotcheff (1971).

Avi Lerner in Cannes.

Randall Emmett in Cannes.

agency'. Would anyone actually wear this? What sort of person would this be?

Melbourne Cup day. I have no interest in horse racing. Horse racing movies can work well, though. Like boxing films, they're easy to understand. The horse that comes in first wins. Other sports can be incomprehensible, or boring, or both, on film. A remarkable exception is the Indian film, *Lagaan*,★ in which a cricket match is so well staged it is actually exciting.

US election day. Still counting.

4th November 2004

Flew to USA. More meetings re *The Contract* on the agenda. Saw three films on the plane. A much better selection than usual. *De-Lovely*, *The Bourne Supremacy* and a morbid but effective film from New Zealand, *In My Father's Den*.

Went straight from airport to the film market in Santa Monica. Hundreds of people buying and selling films. As a general rule, the more elaborate the posters and more expensively designed the promotional material the less impressive the movie. Ran into Michael Ohoven, who said he's ready to do Paul Pender's script — the one where Michael sold his German investors on a title, then had to

---

★ A four-hour film, directed by Ashutosh Gowariker (2001).

find a story to go with it. I pointed out I hadn't heard from him for months and am now more or less committed to *The Contract*. Vincent De Ville was running around, still trying to drum up money for *Semmelweiss*, though he's told me many times he already has it. Also saw Avi Lerner and Randall Emmett. Avi's company has more films in production than any Hollywood studio. At least 15 films are shooting simultaneously. No one seems to know where his financing comes from and few, if any, of the films make it into the theatres. Avi is tall and handsome with thick curly grey hair and is full of charm. The charm is a worry. I tend to shy away from people who are professionally ingratiating.

5th November 2004

Avi Lerner's office — with Boaz Davidson, J.D. Zeik and others. Boaz — a courteous Israeli aged around 60 — has some good script notes for *The Contract*. But he's had the script for a month, so why didn't he give them to me before? Thinking about this, the reason is probably because he's the only person in Avi's company who reads the scripts. This means he's got to deal not only with the ones they're committed to, but all the material that keeps arriving.

Met with Kevin Costner in the Polo lounge at The Beverly Hills Hotel. This hotel was closed for a couple of years while it was being rebuilt. When it opened again it was exactly the same. I found Costner in the restaurant, drinking soup. He was friendly and direct. Immediately told me he has no interest whatever in acting in *The Contract* as he has a film he wants to direct, but wanted to meet me. He recently saw *Don's Party* on TV and was very impressed. Said it was late at night and he assumed at first it was a porn movie as he'd never heard of it, or of any of the actors involved.*

Dinner at Evzen Kolar's. A borrowed house in Venice. The owner is photographer Richard D'Amore,† and there are pictures of luscious naked girls over the walls. Bright crowd at the party, all moaning about Kerry losing the election, very similar to the Latham crowd in Sydney. I don't think anyone on the east or west coast of the USA votes for Bush, but there are a lot of people living in-between.

6th November 2004

J.D. Zeik has flown in from the east coast. We work all day on the script of *The Contract*. Can it ever be made plausible? The story is quite absurd from around the

---

* *Don's Party* was made in Sydney in 1977. Leading actors were John Hargreaves, Graham Kennedy, Graeme Blundell, Jeanie Drynan and Ray Barrett.

† About a year later, his wife shot him dead then committed suicide. Evidently she believed — wrongly — he was about to leave her for another woman.

halfway mark. I mentioned this to Barry Humphries who said, 'Well, *Casablanca* doesn't make any sense.' True enough, but *Casablanca* had a bunch of appealing actors, good dialogue (the dialogue in *The Contract* is still hopelessly dull) with a number of really memorable lines (most of them in the original play on which the film script was based) and a romantic triangle, Bogart/Bergman/Henreid, that was goofy but appealing.

At Zabar's deli met English producer Barnaby Thompson about the Nöel Coward project, *Easy Virtue*. Agreed we'd give the script to Uma Thurman. Whatever happened to the copy that went to Diane Lane? Did she ever respond? I suppose no response is a response.

7th November 2004

Breakfast with an actor friend. He recently made a film in Europe and fell madly in love with his leading lady — and she with him, or so he thought. He came back to LA, told his wife he was leaving (but didn't mention another woman — evidently he employed the old trick of 'just wanting some space'), then went back to London, where, to his surprise, the leading lady was quite distant and took evasive action. It took him a month to realise she didn't want to continue the affair, let alone marry him. He spent hours on the phone with his therapist. Lost 30 pounds in weight. He went back to his wife.

Then — Pieter Kroonenburg about the Chet Baker project. Still insists he has the finance, but we have to see what's happening with *The Contract*. My agent tells me the agreement we have commits me to the film, although I'll bet that if the production company decide they don't want to go ahead I'll be left without any fee. All of these independent films are precarious. The money often comes through at the last minute, if at all. If I like the projects I have to take them seriously and invest a lot of time with script revisions, location surveys, etc — all for no fee. If I don't do this I can pretty well guarantee the project WON'T happen. My commitment can be the factor that drags the finance, screaming and yelling, over the line.

8th November 2004

Met Alex Schwartz at Walden Media. She gave me two scripts on the William Wilberforce project by different writers, which she says they intend to make. I have to read them and make notes.

Stage Beauty, with Claire Danes and Billy Crudup. Well directed by Richard Eyre and shot by Andrew Dunn. Crudup has never become a big star; somehow he's managed to remain almost unknown despite leading roles in a number of films and a talent to equal that of Russell Crowe. Evidently Crudup left his 8-month pregnant wife for Claire Danes during the shoot. Not commendable, but understandable. What a gorgeous creature she is.

9th November 2004

Amended script arrives for *The Contract* from J.D. Zeik. I check it through. He's done a good job considering the short time. I still think the inclusion of the grandfather is a mistake and the characters still all speak in much the same manner. Sent it to Randall to forward to Costner. Randall insists Costner is still interested, even though I've told everyone this is definitely not the case. They think he's playing hard to get. Could be right. I've seen actors finally agree to roles they initially rejected, just through being hounded.

Saw Peter Rawley★ about the Nadine Gordimer novel *The House Gun*, which he wants me to adapt — for a modest fee. BUT he insists he can raise the money for the film. Don't know . . . The novel is superbly written but won't be easy to script. A murder story, with social implications, and the murderer is known from the beginning, which will weaken tension.

★ An ex-agent, English — now a producer.

10th November 2004

Breakfast with Bruce Greenwood.* He's giving one of his kidneys to his mother. It's a four-month recovery period — for him. Hope it all works out OK, for both of them. Greenwood must be one of the most pleasant (and talented) actors I've worked with. Very amiable, agreeable and with a lively interest in people other than himself.

Did notes on the Colin Welland version of the Wilberforce story. A better script than the other version, though the story flounders in the centre. Wilberforce seems to have been a real goody-goody. Must try and find some flaws to make him more interesting.

11th November 2004

Meeting with Randall Emmett and others at Avi Lerner's office. Hard to pin Randall down to talk as he's hyperactive and keeps running around to other offices, or takes endless calls on his mobile. They think they have Costner and Freeman, though Costner wants $10 million (!!!) instead of the $8 million they're offering, while Morgan will work for $5 million only if Costner is getting $5 million! They think this can be resolved.

---

* He played a major role in *Double Jeopardy*.

Lunch with Vincent De Ville re *Semmelweiss*. He now realises, at last, that they need a new script. I could rewrite it, I'm sure, but it would take a month. I don't have this time now. Despite the claims of finance, there wouldn't be anything available for the script rewrite.

Barnaby Thompson tells me he's sent the Noël Coward script to Uma Thurman and Bill Nighy.

In Rabineau's office I overhear him talking on the phone to Terry Gilliam, telling him about the western script by the actress Madeleine Stowe, which I'd turned down. I think it is awful, but evidently Fox Searchlight paid $2 million for it and it's the hottest property in town. Either I'm wrong about it or they are. I think they are.

Ray, about Ray Charles. Well played by Jamie Foxx. Fascinating story, though too long. Most films are too long. How does this happen? Every time I have a preview the audience is quick to be critical of sequences that are indulgent. This is followed up by the producers insisting on cuts. Yet I often see films that are too long by 30 to 40 minutes. Don't they have previews?

12th November 2004

Breakfast with John Papsidera, a casting director. Asked him to read *Semmelweiss* and give Vincent a hand with the casting. Unless Vincent pays him some money (unlikely) I doubt if he'll do anything. Why should he? Vincent says he has money so this should be an interesting test.

Suddenly an urgent call from Randall Emmett to pay a quick visit to Steven Seagal. Not sure why, but I suspect he might've heard about the remarks I made about his eccentricities in my Gold Coast lecture. I have a vision of my body being tied into a knot — Seagal started off as a martial arts advisor to the acting community.

Seagal's house is in Brentwood. A rambling place with 15 cars parked out the front — but all inside the gates. A number of people are hanging around both inside and outside the house.

Steven has yet another action movie to do for Avi Lerner, though he doesn't look too fit. He's huge, around 6 foot 5, but flabby. Hair badly dyed jet black. Evidently he wants a role away from the action films, but it won't happen. He's too embedded in them. He's not had a film released in theatres for some years, but there is evidently a big market (Australia being one of the best) for his movies on DVD. He talked about playing a role, even a small one, in *The Contract*. I told him there is no role to play. If he was one of the baddies pursuing Morgan Freeman through the forest it would unbalance the whole movie, just because of the screen character Seagal has created. Brosnan and Connery could escape James Bond, but I doubt if Seagal can slip away from his martial arts background. Foreground, rather.

As we spoke an Asian girl hovered by his elbow. From time to time she was sent off with a whispered message to do something or other. She returned and whispered into Steven's ear.

Luckily, there was no reference to my Gold Coast remarks. I guess he doesn't read papers from Coolangatta.

George Furla* took me to see his modelling agency in Beverly Hills. Hundreds of photos of beautiful girls are all over the walls. George tells me he and Randall set the place up just so they could meet girls. Elaborate, but effective. I meet their manager, who is an ebullient Australian. He seems very happy. No wonder. He's meeting all the girls, too.

Then to Walden Media again to meet yet more people to discuss *Wilberforce*. Four young women among them, *de rigueur* in Hollywood these days. Not sure who any of them are except for the well-known producer Ed Pressman, a quiet man who doesn't say much. Just nods and smiles. They all have my notes by now. I tell them I prefer Colin Welland's script and advise he does a rewrite. But evidently he's so slow they didn't think it worthwhile. I recommended Tim Prager. Don't know how they'll react to that.

They invested in *Ray*, which I tell them I liked apart from the over-sentimental final dream scene where the grown-up Ray Charles visits his mother. Maudlin stuff. There is a shocked silence as they all declare it their favourite scene and the favourite of all the test audiences.

---

* A business partner of Randall Emmett. Quite different in character. George is reticent and softly spoken.

Dinner at the House of Blues on Sunset Boulevard with Kevin Marcy.* He'd called me to say he wants to make a film about the woman who posed for the Rolls Royce emblem. (A model named Eleanor Thornton, who was the mistress of Lord Montagu and died in 1915 when a ship they were travelling on to India collected a German torpedo. Montagu survived.) The outline is interesting, but it seems likely that Kevin is another one of those people with no finance whatever. Maybe the sheer number of these people around is teaching me a bit of caution at last. He asks me to recommend a writer. I suggest my old friend Peter Buchman, an English writer with some good TV drama credits and a couple of novels.

13th November 2004

Talked with a salesman about buying a Blackberry so I can have the same phone number all over the world. He was cagey about the charges outside the USA. I phoned Stephen Endelman,† who I knew had bought a Blackberry. He told me that he'd used his in Europe but then had such huge bills when he'd returned to America that he threw the thing away.

---

* Associate producer on *Scary Movie 3* (2003) and *The Naked Gun* (1998).

† A composer — he wrote the music for *Evelyn* and *Bride of the Wind* — and friend.

Saw Pieter Kroonenburg again and tell him I'll do the Chet Baker film if the deal isn't done with Costner by mid-week. (I'd much rather do the Chet project but my agent tells me I'm legally attached to *The Contract*.) Does Kroonenburg have the money? He insists that both Colin Farrell and Jim Carrey (!) are interested in playing Chet. Could this be true? Kroonenburg is a handsome Dutchman of around 60. He has produced a few films and people I've spoken to about him respect him. On the other hand he hasn't produced a film for over six years . . .

14th November 2004

In a Santa Monica hotel, I meet Jerry Zeitman, an old-time producer, who gives me a script, *Adventures in Darkness*, which he says is financed. About a blind boy. Zeitman has an attractive 42-year-old wife, though he must be in his late seventies.

Lunch with a writer friend, recently married, who feels he is drowning in domesticity. Says his wife watches him very closely. He is trying to think of a way he can escape for a few hours to see a young woman he met in Borders. A popular pick-up place, he tells me. He insists that Nicole Kidman once propositioned him there. I'm very dubious about this. Possible, though. I had a friend in London who picked up vast numbers of foreign girls in the National Gallery. Evidently it was quite easy to strike up a conversation while admiring a painting, preferably one with acres of nudes. Browsing books in Borders could be somewhat similar.

A 10.30 pm flight back to Australia.

Australian film *Somersault* on the plane. Intense, low key and quite brilliantly done with a highly polished script that pulls all it's strands together without being obvious or corny. Abbie Cornish and Sam Worthington in the leads, but superbly acted by everyone involved. I love the final conversation in the car which draws the parallel, so subtly, between the town drowned under the lake and the suppressed emotions of the film's characters.

19th November 2OO4

Sydney. Cleaning up study, answering mail, reading scripts.

A typically high-speed message from Randall Emmett to say that Costner will definitely let us know tomorrow! They've agreed to pay him $10 million and to finance his next film. Actors like him are so wealthy the money is trivial. He won't be swayed by a mere $10 million and he could easily get the finance for any film he wants to do, even after the disaster of *The Postman*. I still think that when he told me he wasn't interested in *The Contract*, he meant it.

Saw *De-Lovely* again. It's much better on the big screen. Really very well directed (by Irwin Winkler) with clever integration of musical numbers into the story. Very moving, if a bit long. I've never heard those Cole Porter songs so well orchestrated and sung, Diana Krall and Vivian Green being the most outstanding.

A call from Peter Buchman. Kevin Marcy has been in touch about the Rolls Royce script, but hasn't offered a fee. He wants a treatment so he can go to a studio to find money. This is infuriating. When I met with Kevin, and he asked me to recommend a writer, he didn't tell me he wanted him to work for nothing.

Heard that Alison Barrett, who cast so many of my films, has died of stomach cancer. A thin, quiet girl, a chain smoker, softly spoken. I was actually at university with her, but despite that, and all the movies we did together, I realise I hardly knew her. I still don't know if she was married or not.

Alison was one of those rare casting directors who didn't see their job as simply supplying a list of every living actor (often with quite a few dead ones thrown in) to the director or even using her position to have lunch with celebrities. She saw all the new plays and movies, read the scripts she was asked to cast, and didn't hesitate to recommend unknowns. When I was looking for a young Australian to play the nurse, a lead role, in *Paradise Road*, Alison suggested Cate Blanchett, who at that time had only done some TV work.

And Ken Hannam died in London. Director of *Sunday Too Far Away* (1975) and many other films. I knew him in Adelaide when I was in pre-production on *Breaker Morant*. We shared an office and I was astonished at his appeal to women, especially as he was around middle-age, short and bald. On one occasion a young actress came in for an interview (for my film, not his). We chatted for a few moments (there wasn't much for her in *Breaker Morant*) and she left. A few minutes later the phone rang and she asked to 'talk to the man sitting at the other desk'. Puzzled, I handed the phone over to Ken. There was a whispered conversation, after which he told me he would be meeting the actress that evening for a drink. Almost apologetically he explained that women had pursued him like that all of his life. Some problem.

An old H.G. Clouzot film, *Quai des Orfèvres* (1947), on DVD. Not too bad, but a bit plodding. Most of those old French films, regarded as classics, don't stand up too well. Probably true of most films of the 1930s and 40s. The films we're doing today will look strange in 20 years or so. I suppose it's because films reflect the era in which they're made. People watch them in a society with certain morés, certain assumptions. These change, but the films don't. Technique changes all the time, too, but I think that dates films less, despite the immense resources of computer special effects. None of this is surprising. Novels and plays go out of date, too.

20th November 2004

A message from LA to say that the deal has not been done with Costner as he has the flu, so the new deadline is Monday. I can't see what difference the flu would make as he knows all the details of the offer so only needs to say 'yes' or 'no' to his agent. Steve Rabineau still thinks it will happen as 'no one else would be foolish enough to pay Costner $10 million'. Pieter Kroonenburg is anxious as he wants an answer on the Chet Baker film.

Walked up to Balmain early with Frankie (our dog). The Italian flower seller has a photo of an old lady on his wagon. I asked who it was and he said it was his mother, in hospital, just before she died. On the day she died, she wanted her hair brushed as she 'wanted to meet God looking her best'.

Working on revisions to *Curlow Creek*.* Wonder if Patrick Duggan has any chance of finding the money for this. He knows nothing about film production. I think he made his money, lots of it, out of horse studs. He is a strange amiable little man, though with a quick temper. He could always hire himself out as a garden gnome if his film career doesn't take off.

Two concerts with Cordelia. First a wind quintet at Sydney Grammar school, then an ACO concert of Baroque music in Angel Place. Both well performed. Angel Place concert hall has good acoustics, but looks as if it's been built on the cheap. There's a temporary look about it.

---

* I delivered the first draft and am now doing a second after some notes from the producers.

Long call from Randall Emmett who says he's convinced the Costner deal will be done on Monday! I've noticed that producers who actually churn out one film after another have the characteristic of absurd optimism. Probably the key to their success. They even manage to put a favourable interpretation on setbacks that would send most people into despair. Though, this time, even the normally cynical Rabineau thinks the deal with Costner will go through. Let's see.

21st November 2004

Sunday. Still working on revisions of *Curlow Creek*. Saw DVD of my old film *Mister Johnson*.* A poor transfer. Seems to be a bootleg copy as it's not been colour corrected and is in the wrong aspect ratio.† Certainly it's not been issued by the American distributor. I still think it's a good film. Did no business at all, anywhere, though it's the best reviewed film I've made. The American previews were disastrous because African–American audience members were hostile about the situation on screen where a young African man (played by Maynard Eziashi) is an office clerk

---

* Filmed in Nigeria in 1991 with Pierce Brosnan. The cast also included Edward Woodward, Beatie Edney and Nick Reding.

† It was shot widescreen but has been transferred to DVD in the old pre-1960 4:3 (nearly square) ratio. This destroys the compositions.

and subordinate to a white District Officer (Pierce Brosnan). No amount of explanation that this was in fact a common situation in West Africa in the 1920s would placate them. I couldn't comprehend the hostility in any case as in no way is the African character belittled.

Dinner with Cordelia and saw the rushes of her new short film.* I know from her previous work that she's a talented photographer and director. I'm rather in awe of her, partly because she's beautiful and has an imperious manner, with me at any rate. I feel intellectually inferior to all my children, for that matter.

22nd November 2004

Suddenly realised I hadn't received my new credit card and ATM card, though I applied for them about six weeks ago. Called in to the bank and found they had no record of the applications. Had to do them both again.

Finalised revisions on *Curlow Creek* and emailed it off. Managed to work in a nude swimming scene. That should make them happy. Today was the deadline for Costner's deal on *The Contract*. Randall Emmett now tells me they want until tomorrow! Pointless. We've already had at least six deadlines and it's perfectly clear Costner doesn't want

---

* The short film, *The Eye Inside*, went on to be screened in a number of film festivals. It won awards for both direction and photography.

to do the film. Actors are invariably incapable of saying 'no' (though Costner was clear enough when I met with him) — usually it's a quick 'yes' or they say nothing. I want to get out of this project now. I'm sick of it. Called Pieter Kroonenburg and told him I'd do the Chet Baker film. He was excited. I just hope he really has the money.*

26th November 2004

Randall Emmett has now given the script to Dennis Quaid. He's supposed to reply after thanksgiving.

Vincent DeVille says he has the money for *Semmelweiss* but it's 'actor contingent', a phrase that means virtually nothing. Almost every film is 'actor contingent', meaning simply that investors will not put up finance until a big name actor is attached. The script is of scant importance, the director of some importance, but rarely enough to guarantee finance with his/her name alone

Vincent has sent his *Semmelweiss* script (now wisely retitled *Fever*) to John Cusack, who I'm sure won't be interested. He must get so many offers to do major films I can't see him considering an independent Hungarian film for a fraction of his normal fee. I sent Vincent a list of suitable actors to play Semmelweiss, Henry Thomas being the best actor and the most suitable for the eponymous

---

* He didn't.

role, but he doesn't have a 'name', so wouldn't even be considered. Vincent also wants to send it to Olivier Martinez. I've agreed, though I think he's too Gallic and too much a romantic leading man. I can't imagine him wanting to play a Hungarian doctor who is beaten to death in an insane asylum! Danny Huston has expressed an interest in the part. He's very talented, but I doubt if the finance gurus would consider him.

Bill Gavin phoned from London to say he thinks he can put *Master Class* together, though he still doesn't have anyone to play Stalin. Michael Gambon more or less agreed to do it but is now tied up on *Harry Potter*. We're to try to think of someone else. Bill asked if I knew Tony Hopkins. I've met him once socially and could only contact his agent — who is unlikely to be helpful. He won't want his client in a low-budget, low-fee film. Perfect actor is Ben Kingsley — but one of the producers doesn't like him(!). Strange, as Kingsley has to be one of the greatest actors alive. Same producer also rejected Sam Neill, another brilliant actor, for Shostakovich.

Bill Gavin is feeling confident because of the success of *Whale Rider*, which he produced in his native New Zealand. He described it to me as 'a $10 million film that looks like a $2 million film'.

Jerry Zeitman called and reiterated that they have the money for *Adventures in Darkness*, the script he gave me about the blind boy. Hmmm. It isn't bad. A true story, written by the central character. How he overcame his disadvantage, etc. Zeitman keeps insisting he has been calling my agent, Steve Rabineau, about a deal but that Rabineau hasn't taken the calls and hasn't phoned back. When I put this all to Rabineau he says he has had no phone calls from Zeitman. What's this all about?

27th November 2004

Steve Rabineau says he's checked and that Zeitman has no finance. Zeitman insists the film *is* financed. Who is correct? What's going on?

Read *The Ridge and the River*, an adaptation of the (overpraised) novel by Tom Hungerford. Sincere, but far too much Aussie slang. The characters all sound the same. Also, far too little action for a war film.

Harold Hopkins called in. Haven't seen him for some years. Somehow he never became the big star I thought he would when he played in *Don's Party* and *The Club*. He now lives up near Wisemans Ferry with very little money. Said he's hardly worked in 15 years. Has never gone on the dole. Feels it's humiliating. He went on a superstrict vegetarian diet some years ago — at one point he ate nothing but carrots. I never thought this did him any good. He aged from a handsome young man to an old one without the intervening middle age. He even forced his dog to become vegetarian. I used to slip the poor thing pieces of meat when Harold wasn't looking.

He told me a horror story of his father committing suicide by blowing out his brains when he found out that four of his seven kids were fathered by a Mr Klug (!) — Harold being one of the four. Harold found the body.

30th November 2004

Steve Rabineau says Dennis Quaid has also 'passed' on *The Contract*. At least we had an answer. No word yet from Randall Emmett. I think they'll give up now — two major actors have turned them down.

Rabineau is talking to Walden about the Wilberforce project. This is something I really want to do. So few really worthwhile projects turn up — or, rather, it's so hard to find finance for them. I must have four or five scripts that would make films equal to the best ones I've done, but haven't been able to raise the money. My lack of business acumen is a great drawback. All I can understand are the broad outlines. What an advantage it would be to know how to piece together a budget from the different sources, how to draw up the contracts to reflect their equity, how to arrange distribution deals that still return something to the film's producers, to understand tax structures and production incentives (rebates) in various countries. Best of all, I think, it would be advantageous to know WHO to go to and WHERE to find them.

1st December 2004

Randall Emmett is *still* talking to Costner (!) who wants script changes! I point out we'd done what he asked — mainly changes to the ending — and if he wants something else done he has to give us notes in writing, so no one can be confused about what it is he's requesting. Also, it'll make it harder for him to move the goalposts.

They're also still talking to Quaid. Have offered to finance a film for him to direct, too. Yet with all this cash available, Avi Lerner's company has made almost nothing that's had a major release.

Rabineau suggests the role is offered to John Cusack. I think they're all floundering. Cusack is a terrific actor but might be too young for the role. He's meant to have a 13-year-old son.

3rd December 2004

Conference call with heads of Walden Films who seem receptive to my idea that I write and direct *Wilberforce*. They will talk with Rabineau on Monday. Good idea, it could make a great film, though they stun me a bit suggesting that the slave trade is never shown as 'it's too horrific'. I point out it will be very difficult to make a film about the man who had it eradicated if it's never seen! It'd be like doing an anti-prizefight film without showing a fight.

Directing John Cusack in *The Contract*.

Now, Randall Emmett, more frantic than ever, tells me that John Cusack *will* do *The Contract*! If true — (did Cusack read the script?) — this could throw a spanner in the works of *Wilberforce*, as my agents will insist I have an inescapable commitment to *The Contract*.

Saw *Lagaan* for the fourth time.* A great film. Full of exuberance and vitality and *joie de vivre*. The choreography of the long cricket match in the final hour is superb. Even the Bollywood songs are engaging.

4th December 2004

Rabineau calls and says he hasn't heard that Cusack will do the film and he's Cusack's agent! Calls back an hour later to say Cusack IS interested but wants $6 million and they've only offered him a measly $4 million — for six weeks work. Cheapskates.

7th December 2004

Randall Emmett says Cusack is fine with the $4 million offer. I tell him Steve Rabineau told me Cusack wants $6 million. Emmett quickly rings off, stunned, saying he'll check it and call back.

---

* Everyone should buy the DVD and see this movie.

A screening of *Puberty Blues** in Paddington as there was a launch of the short book Nell Schofield wrote about the making of the film — in which she had the leading role. Not many people there, but Geoff Rhoe and Jad Capelja† turned up. Jad and Nell were only around 17 when we shot the movie. We found them, for the leading roles, after quite a long search. I was astonished at the time at the lack of interest teenagers had in being in the film. Alison Barrett was calling everyone she knew in Sydney and Melbourne to try and scrape up the cast of around eight kids. I recall addressing a bunch of them together. They seemed mildly interested, though this dissipated when they found out the shoot was six weeks long. The boys all wanted to go surfing up the coast. I don't know what the girls wanted to do, but acting in a film didn't have much attraction. I wonder if the situation would be different today? Probably would. Everyone seems to want to act or direct.

I didn't watch the film through, only the opening titles; enough to see it was an old copy with totally faded colour. Probably unavoidable. Colour prints only last 10 to 15 years. After that they turn brown or just look washed out. Now, with digital technology, they can be restored, although it's expensive.

Cusack is to phone me on Saturday.

----

* I directed this film in Sydney in 1981. It's adapted from a novel by Kathy Lette and Gabrielle Carey.

† Both teenage actors in *Puberty Blues* (1981).

Told Randall Emmett, again, that pre-production time is desperately short if they want to film in February. Like most money men he has absolutely no idea of what goes into making a film — location surveys, casting of all the minor roles, finding the technicians, etc.

8th December 2004

Email from Sheryl Crown re *The Dead Wait*, saying she wants to do it for less than $2 million! Budget has dropped from $8 million; she can't get any investment at that figure. I said no. I've cut budgets before but this is ridiculous, especially as it's set during a war and would need a lot of special effects. I cut the budget of *Driving Miss Daisy* from $17 million to $7.5 million by drastically reducing the shooting days, filming on location instead of sets and agreeing to defer my modest director's fee. At least I collected it when the film, to the astonishment of all, turned out to be a hit.

Randall Emmett is talking about pushing *The Contract* back to May and shooting in Canada! I'm not keen on further delays, to put it mildly.

Asked Steve Rabineau if I can get out of *The Contract* entirely, but he insists the film is going ahead and I have a deal that would involve me in legal action if I try to withdraw. This means I lose *Wilberforce*. Disastrous.

Spent a day working with Tony Buckley and Peter Yeldham on *Drylands* script. Went OK. They seemed to agree with a lot of my notes, most of which relate to making the basic story from the novel a bit more logical.

12th December 2004

Working on proposal for Discovery Channel; a documentary about Australia. Watched a number of these that have been done (some American and one French one) recently and was amazed at their similarity. It seems there is a limited range of subject matter common to all of them ... surf carnivals, outback road trains, outback characters, crocodiles, cattle mustering. I don't basically object to all this, it's just that it's a strange emphasis for a country in which at least three-quarters of the population live in big cities. I wouldn't mind including something about Australia's Nobel prize winners (there are 11 of them) and about the problems facing the country now because of over use of resources, etc. Should contact Tim Flannery, who seems to have written almost all the books on Australia's natural history, flora, fauna, ecological and social problems.

Meeting at Beyond studios in Artarmon. Everyone very pleasant and bright, though I was a bit startled at a suggestion that we link all the sequences in the film with a water motif, that is, the camera goes down into water in one place and pops up in another. As there is a frightening shortage of water everywhere in the country, this seems to me to be sending out the wrong message.

Spoke to Peter James* about the Beyond documentary. He advised against getting involved in TV. He says the director has no control. The film is made by a committee. An odd way to work. Novels and plays aren't written by committees. Nor is music composed by a committee — with the exception of the 'Yellow River Concerto'.

At a Christmas drinks party, I chatted to a lady who has a friend who was Max Aitken's (Lord Beaverbrook) mistress for years — until he died. She was described as a 'good' mistress, that is, she caused no problem for the family and didn't contest the will — out of which she got nothing. Aitken had given her a flat in Knightsbridge, which she still has — and very little else. Now she's over 60 and 'no one wants a mistress of that age'.

15th December 2004

Two days kayaking at André Fleuren's place at Hardys Bay. Went on a long walk — an hour — down a steep path to a beach. Exhausting. The place is so hard to reach, the beach is almost deserted. A few nude swimmers. Why are these always ugly old guys? Why don't beautiful young women go nude swimming?

---

* Australian cameraman. Has shot nearly all of my films since, and including, *Driving Miss Daisy*.

Evening. Watched *Being Julia* on DVD. Not very good, though Annette Bening seems totally English. The film is uncertain in tone. I think it's meant to be light and amusing, though it's neither. István Szabó is a gifted director, but his English isn't particularly good. It's so difficult to direct actors in a language imperfectly spoken. All those American films by Louis Malle* were very odd. Nowhere near as good as his French movies and I'm sure it's because he was unaware of so many nuances in English.

Also watched Robert Benton's† first film as director, *Bad Company* (1972), a well-written story of two boys drifting into a life as outlaws after they draft-dodge during the Civil War. Great performance from Jeff Bridges. This film had tepid reviews when it was released but strikes me as one of the best westerns ever made — compares favourably with *My Darling Clementine* (1946), *Stagecoach* (1939) and *3.10 to Yuma* (1957).

18th December 2004

Rabineau says the battle is continuing over John Cusack's fee for *The Contract*. If the film's start is pushed back then Morgan Freeman is no longer available and

---

* *Alamo Bay* (1985), *Atlantic City* (1980), *Crackers* (1984), etc.

† American writer and director. Won an Academy Award for *Kramer vs Kramer* (1979).

that role has to be recast. All a nightmare. Meanwhile there is an offer from Walden to write and direct *Wilberforce* — a more attractive proposition as it could be a major film. Amazing to me that no one has touched this subject before.

Reading Prescott's *History of the Conquest of Peru*. Incredible that Pizarro conquered a strong military empire with 140 men. The Indians were terrified of his guns and horses. He took the Inca (or ruler) prisoner after persuading him to visit unarmed. Then agreed to release him in exchange for a roomful of gold. The gold was delivered but he still executed the Inca. A few centuries later, Pizarro would've made a good studio executive, or agent.

Prescott was quite astonishing, too. Although this book and *History of the Conquest of Mexico* were both written in the 19th century, they've not been eclipsed by later works on the same subjects. AND Prescott was blind. Had to have all the research material read to him.

21st December 2004

Flew up to Byron Bay for a week. Rented a large house, not far from the beach. Very crowded here.

23rd December 2004

Λ call on the mobile from Randall Emmett, who is in Florida. Normally his calls are only a few seconds long. There is a short burst of information, usually wrong, then a curt 'bye' and 'call you later'. This time I couldn't get him off the phone. Says the deal for *The Contract* is signed with Morgan Freeman *and* John Cusack, with shooting to begin in May, in Romania. So ... I mustn't pull out of the film and sign for *Wilberforce*. I've already tried to do this, and failed. Rabineau even uses the argument that *Wilberforce* isn't financed, though I am convinced it is.

Saw *Sideways* on DVD — two friends take a week to have a wine tour in California before one of them (a small-time actor) is to be married. Well done, well played and directed (Alexander Payne) with a sure touch. Often very funny, with only one or two moments that don't quite ring true. Payne must be one of the few directors around who doesn't shoot everything in huge close ups — something that's been forced onto us by the studio execs who watch dailies on small screens and can't see anything except the close shots.

Payne has a wonderful sense of place and a great eye for contemporary America. The highways, cafés, motels, etc. Everyone photographs these things but somehow his viewpoint makes them more than mere backdrops to the dialogue. They become part of the fabric of the story and characters. Interestingly, he doesn't seem to be taking the easy route by ridiculing all the urban ugliness. He seems to be fascinated by it as part of the modern landscape, or cityscape. Through careful compositions he even finds a kind of beauty in it, much as Jeffrey Smart does in his paintings.

25th December 2004

Christmas with Cordelia, Dirk,* his parents — Gunther and Heida — Virginia, Trilby and John Duigan (V's brother). Hot weather. Lots of swimming, bush walks and kayaking.

27th December 2004

Now I've officially lost the Wilberforce film. They're moving on to their second choice, they tell me.† Despite my immense enthusiasm for this project, I've been steered relentlessly towards *The Contract*. I suspect my agency hung on so tenaciously as they represent both the leading actors and can see huge commissions coming their way.

---

* Cordelia's husband, a young German architect.

† The film has now been made, directed by Michael Apted, under the title *Amazing Grace* (2006).

Another call from Jerry Zeitman, *again* saying he has put in a firm offer on *Adventures in Darkness* but never heard back from Rabineau. Rabineau says he's *never* had a call from him. Incredibly strange situation. One of them must be lying. But which one? And why? It certainly doesn't make sense that Zeitman would keep telling me he's calling my agent if in fact he's never done so. On the other hand, Rabineau could be saying there's been no calls simply because he doesn't want any projects considered other than *The Contract*, though this behaviour seems out of character. Also, his assistant, who keeps a list of every call made in and out of the office, has also assured me there have been no calls from Zeitman.

Saw Mel Gibson's *The Passion of the Christ*. Well made, as are most films these days, but just an excuse for a vast excess of violence, performed on Christ by an overdrawn bunch of leering, vicious Roman legionnaires. Mel is obsessed with torture and flagellation scenes. (*Braveheart* was similar.) Great lighting by Caleb Deschanel, and with some good touches — a sinister Devil. Good performance from James Caviezel, whose look they've taken from that corny painting of Christ that is reproduced all over the world.

Mel has had, is having, an incredible career. Not only is he a top-flight movie star, but he is easily the most successful Australian director, with at least two huge hits (*Braveheart* and *The Passion*), and is the only Australian to have actually won the Academy Award for Best Director.

31st December 2004

Four days ago a vast tsunami, caused by an earthquake near Sumatra, devastated seaside towns all through that part of Asia. From merely hundreds, they're now reporting about 100,000 dead. Already there's been a newspaper article saying the US base in Diego Garcia knew about the giant wave but said nothing as Bush wants to wipe out the Moslems in Indonesia. Australia is a great country for these conspiracy theories. My favourite is the one about former Prime Minister Harold Holt — who disappeared while swimming — actually being a spy for the Chinese! I was told by a group of journalists, in all seriousness, that he was picked up off the coast by a Chinese submarine and is now living in Beijing. At least the film business doesn't have all the ratbags.

With Trilby and Virginia drove up to Noosa from Byron Bay. This place is definitely the Bel Air of Queensland. Lavish houses and expensive restaurants. We have managed to find ourselves the only unattractive apartment in town. Nestled between two hills, it's cleverly positioned to avoid the sun at all times.

Australia has changed so much. I remember beach resorts as a child. A few ramshackle fibro beach houses and a milk bar that sold hamburgers. Olive oil, foccacia and salads were totally unknown. When I was at university I found out about oil and vinegar salad dressing and tried to persuade my mother that it was preferable to the tomato sauce she poured over lettuce. I failed.

Visited a craft market in a Disneyfied town, Eumundi, a few miles from Noosa. I bought a belt from a stallholder, who recognised me. This happens very rarely. In fact, this was only the third time in my career. The stallholder then proceeded to tell me he was a writer and would like to send me a script. With slight reluctance, I gave him my address. You never know what you'll come across. John Galsworthy was on a cruise when the second mate asked him if he'd mind reading a book he'd written. Galsworthy — then a hugely celebrated writer — graciously agreed, despite his trepidation. The second mate was Joseph Conrad and the novel was *Almayer's Folly*. A masterpiece. Similarly, Dvořák was on holiday in rural Czechoslovakia when he overheard a local playing some piano music. Struck by its quality, he knocked on the door of the house it came from and asked what it was. He was told it was a local composer, Janáček.

New Year's Eve at David* and Kristin Williamson's house by the beach. Despite my strongly expressed opposition, I was forced into karaoke singing. My efforts produced immense hilarity as I struggled through the 'Banana Boat Song', though I don't think I was notably worse than anyone else.

---

* I filmed two of his plays, *Don's Party* and *The Club*. He also wrote the script for Peter Weir's *Gallipoli* (1981).

At one point in the evening some local louts threw bottles over a fence. They landed dangerously among David's guests. He immediately exploded and yelled to the louts to desist. If not, they were welcome to come in and fight him. Not one of them took up the challenge. David obviously has physical courage to match his moral and intellectual abilities. He was undeterred by the fact the louts next door must've been at least 30 years younger than him.

7th January 2005

A message from Rabineau's office confirming the deal on *The Contract* is all agreed. No backing out now. I suppose I shouldn't complain. I always wanted to be a film director. Spoke to Avi Lerner, who said we should shoot in Romania in May. Wants me to go over in February to find locations.

23rd January 2005

Now that *The Contract* is going ahead, all the other projects seem to be coming through. As well as *Wilberforce*, Barnaby Thompson tells me he has the finance for *Easy Virtue*. Just my luck. He won't wait for

me to finish the other film. He'll find another director.*
I know I'd be much better handling these two films
than the thriller.

A week in Bangkok at the film festival where I am
president of the Jury. This is all pretty easy to take. We
(the Jury) are staying in a luxury hotel by the river,
(unsurprisingly named the Oriental) voted, I've been
told, the No. 1 hotel in the world. At breakfast, outdoors,
I ran into my old friend, the Italian cameraman Dante
Spinotti,† who shot *Crimes of the Heart* for me. His first
American film, I believe. Dino De Laurentiis had seen
his work in an Italian sword and sandals epic and
recognised his talent, so imported him to America. Dante
is the least typical Italian I've met. Quietly spoken (with
near-perfect English), witty and unassuming, and a calm
manner that never deserts him. He is in Bangkok giving
lectures on photography.

The car that takes us to the first screening, somewhere
in the middle of the city, is hopelessly bogged down in
traffic. The journey stretches into a couple of hours. There
must be something easier. I am told that the trip on the
new above-ground rail link is only a couple of minutes.
From now on we dispense with the car.

---

* With all the delays and confusion over *The Contract*, I lost this project.
Certainly one of Coward's best plays, it is to be directed by Stephan Elliot.

† Dante's credits include *The Last of the Mohicans* (1992), *LA Confidential*
(1997), and *The Insider* (1999).

The screening room itself turns out to be the most luxurious I've ever seen. We are all seated in huge padded armchairs that recline at the touch of a button, making it easy to doze off during the more dreary films.

Actually, none of the films qualify as dreary — *The Sea Inside*, *Motorcycle Diaries*, *The Chorus*, *Zelary*, *Old Boy* (well made but obscure Korean film), *Red Dust* (South African), *The Syrian Bride* (Israeli — only so-so). Mike Leigh film, *Vera Drake*, was rather ponderous but skilfully directed. *Being Julia* is no better on the big screen, but I am alone in not caring for it. The Italian film, *Don't Move*, was the only real disaster. Absurd story of a doctor and his (improbable) affair with a tart. Lugubrious.

At the hotel, one of the American guests is taking a bunch of people, including some teenage girls, to a porn show in a nightclub. I am unenthusiastic about the idea and I'm sure they all go off branding me as a hopeless old conservative.

28th January 2005

Sydney. Suggested to Avi's company that he meet my old friend Richard Rothschild as he'd be an ideal line producer for *The Contract*. They met, then Richard had a message from them that they thought his 'quote was too high'. He pointed out he'd not yet given them a quote. Odd, as they seem to have no other suggestions for a line producer. I suspect they have someone in mind and agreed to meet RR just to humour me.

Tell Rabineau they pay the US$25,000 development fee, which they've owed for six months, or I withdraw. An email said they'd pay. But they've agreed to this before and not paid. Interesting to see if they do. If they don't pay by the end of the week, I can legally escape from the project.

A concert at the Opera House of Leonard Cohen songs; they are much better when he isn't singing them. Linda Thompson (Steve Kenis' wife) was one of the singers. An adrogynous singer named Anthony Hegarty is quite outstanding. His performance of 'If it be your Will' elicits a wildly enthusiastic audience response.

A message to say that Cate Blanchett now wants to do *Miss Potter* having seen *Finding Neverland*, though I can't imagine how that insipid film inspired her. She's supposed to call me, though I doubt if she will. Actors rarely make calls to directors. They work through their agents.

4th February 2005

No call from Cate Blanchett. I'm sure Mike Medavoy, the producer, will be quite happy to be able to replace me as director now that I'm tied up on *The Contract*. Ever since Medavoy became involved in this project I've never felt that he wanted me to direct it, though he's never actually said this. Something in his rather disengaged manner has always made me feel that he'd edge me out if he could.* A bit tricky for him as the writer brought the script to me in the first place. I've been in the awkward situation a few times where I was engaged for a project but it was then decided somewhere, by someone, that some other director would be preferable. Mostly, I've been lucky and in constant demand, but it's hardly surprising that not everyone likes my films. Some years ago, I was to direct a very funny script by Neil Simon called *The Marrying Man*. I was edged out by the simple procedure of having my desk removed from the office where we were doing the pre-production. I also found it very difficult to find anyone to talk to. They all managed to disappear. Needless to say, I didn't collect any fee at all on either film. I was quite pleased when *The Marrying Man* was a disaster and *An Unfinished Life* disappointing.

The Contract producers pay the development fee, unfortunately.

Max Hastings (who recognised me in the market near Noosa and sent me a script, *Inland from the Sea*) turns out

---

* The Beatrix Potter film has been made with Renée Zellweger and was directed by the Australian Chris Noonan, who made *Babe*. The first I knew that I was no longer director on this project was a short piece in the *Sydney Morning Herald*. I called Mike Medavoy's office and was told they thought I was no longer available. Nonsense. Obviously it was one of those odd situations where someone suddenly decided I may not be the best director for the project.

234

to be a talented writer. Evidently he had some plays performed in Melbourne a few years ago. The script is bizarre and funny. It could be made cheaply as there are only half a dozen characters. The setting is restricted, too. A shack by a deserted beach. Gave it to James Vernon to read. He claims to have a contract to shoot six low-budget films in New Zealand.

Watched Almodovar's *Bad Education*, but the relentless gay encounters are too difficult for me. Then tried *Finding Neverland* again, because of the worldwide euphoria it has generated. It still seems very lame to me; badly cast and badly paced. Two twee for words. I guess Johnny Depp is talented, but I somehow can't get wildly enthusiastic about him. In this film he is absolutely nothing like J.M. Barrie (whose Scottish accent must've been more convincing, too) physically, though I suppose this doesn't matter all that much. Who but a few academics and types like me would have any idea what Barrie looked like? And that's because some years ago I read Andrew Birkin's book on Barrie — *The Lost Boys*.

Viewed *Maria, Full of Grace*, written and directed by Joshua Marston, on the new coded DVD player sent from Los Angeles,* the idea being that the disc won't play on anything else, so there's not much chance of piracy of the nominated films. Won't work. The pirates always find a

---

* Every year the Academy sends films to Academy members on DVD, hoping for their votes for the Academy Awards.

way around these things. Anyway, it's a tough film about a Columbian girl smuggling drugs into the USA. Very well acted by the entire cast. In Spanish, with an American director. He must speak Spanish fluently or he'd never have been able to get such performances.

5th February 2005

My script outline for the Discovery Channel documentary about Australia has been judged — by the head office in Washington — to be too bleak. Now I have to do revisions. I know I was influenced by the books of Tim Flannery (*The Future Eaters*) and Jared Diamond (*Collapse*) — both of which predict a grim future because of deforestation, increasing salinity of the soil, lack of water due to climate change, and overpopulation in relation to resources. In fact, both men claim that the optimum population for the country is 17 million. Diamond analyses various societies that have collapsed over the centuries, many of them, frighteningly, being quite aware of what was going to happen (Easter Island, the Mayans) but doing nothing about it. His vote for the next society to collapse is Australia, followed by China. I think all of this would be far more interesting than yet another film centred around the surf carnival syndrome. Depressingly, I gather there is also little interest in my proposals to include sections on the composer Ross Edwards, the novelist Chris Koch and the remarkable Dr Fiona Wood,* who has developed a revolutionary new treatment — instantly adopted worldwide — for treating burns.

Quite tricky dealing with executives I haven't spoken to. I suggested including a sequence with an Aboriginal dance group and was told this was of no interest. Then the executive suddenly changed and the Aboriginal dances were back on the agenda.

8th February 2005

Love for 3 Oranges at Sydney Opera House. Not my favourite Prokofiev. The audience seemed to enjoy it though. Australians like their humour broad. (I almost always find this resistable, though *Kath and Kim* is funny.) A silly fantasy story designed to look like the movie version of *The Wizard of Oz*. Laboured. Effeminate chorus very irritating.

Dinner with the Los Angeles based conductor George Doherty, who is in Australia conducting a concert of Bugs Bunny cartoon music. Can't imagine anything worse. Who could be interested in listening to two hours of boopy boo music? Thousands of people evidently. All the performances are packed.

---

* Australian of the Year in 2005.

10th February 2005

Richard Rothschild emailed to say Avi Lerner's office told him the start date for *The Contract* is July, not June and that they want him (RR) to line produce. Rabineau emailed and said it's June, not July, and they *don't* want RR.

Clive James has been in Sydney for a few days giving lucrative talks to some group or other. I took him to the airport. He's looking older, and couldn't be tango dancing as much these days as he's put on weight. He's as sharp as ever, though, and as witty. Seems to know quite a bit about any subject that comes up. Annoying. He read a couple of Trilby's short stories and gave her some advice. Sounded sensible to me, but I'm not sure she was impressed. I think she regards anyone over 30 as passé.

12th February 2005

Meeting at Opera office with Richard Hickox, Adrian Collette and Stuart Maunder to discuss directing a production for Opera Australia.* I suggest *Of Mice and Men.*† Stuart has heard the work and thinks it outstanding,

---

* Richard Hickox is chief conductor with Opera Australia. He conducted the *Rigoletto* I directed in Los Angeles. Adrian Collette is chief executive of Opera Australia and Stuart Mauder is an outstanding opera director.

† The opera version. Libretto and music by Carlisle Floyd.

With a model of the set for *A Streetcar Named Desire*. (© Newspix/Alan Pryke)

but they all seem hesitant. Probably worried about finding an audience for it, although I don't think this would be such a problem as the book is so well known. As alternatives, suggested *Tale of Two Cities* (Arthur Benjamin*) and *Sir John in Love* (Vaughan Williams). I've only heard a couple of arias from the Benjamin opera, but it was a big hit at Covent Garden in the 1950s. It'd be an interesting one to stage, partially as Benjamin is an Australian composer. The Vaughan Williams really is a masterpiece and has never been performed in this country; not too much anywhere else either. I guess Verdi's *Falstaff* has always taken precedence. Richard asks if I've heard André Previn's *Streetcar Named Desire*. I saw the original production in San Francisco. Not a bad suggestion.†

Called a friend in LA who has had surgery. I assumed it was something cosmetic, but he said 'I have a new arsehole'.

21st February 2005

In Sofia, Bulgaria. Arrived a few days ago for pre-production on *The Contract*. All signed at last, with Morgan Freeman and John Cusack in the leads. Still a

---

*   Australian composer (1893–1960), now forgotten. Wrote many operas and did the *Stormclouds Cantata* for Hitchcock's *The Man Who Knew Too Much* (1934).

†   I'm directing this opera for the Australian Opera in 2007.

number of smaller, though substantial, roles to cast. I thought we were to film in Romania, but when I checked the ticket it was to Sofia, not Bucharest. I guess it's cheaper here.

Met at the airport by a tall, good-looking, middle-aged man named Bob Misiorowski. He introduced himself as the line producer. Evidently he's produced a number of films for Avi Lerner's company, and directed a few as well. He said that Avi was supposed to call me and let me know of his appointment. There was no call. I assume Avi didn't feel like explaining why they went through all the business with Richard Rothschild.

We spend days rushing around looking at locations and studios. Bob has produced two films here in Bulgaria and knows his way around. Seems odd to be doing a film here that's set in the USA, but a lot have already been done, though most of them were straight to DVD. Now with *The Contract*, *The Black Dahlia*, *The Wicker Man* and *16 Blocks*, Avi is trying to lift his game. These are much bigger budgets with big stars. Not that I've any idea what my budget is. I've never seen one, although my lawyer has repeatedly requested a copy. I've never made a film without seeing and being able to study a budget, but have a feeling I won't be getting one this time, even though it's stipulated in the contract.

Sofia is run-down but being restored. The centre of the city, around the huge cathedral built by the Russians circa 1905, has been largely refurbished with money from the

World Heritage Fund. I know very little about the history of the country — only that the Turks controlled it for hundreds of years. The Russians were instrumental in throwing them out around 1900, but then the Bulgarians were stuck with them and only got rid of them after the fall of the Berlin Wall. I'm told that Sofia was very badly damaged during the war as the Bulgarians changed sides. First they were bombed by the Russians, Americans and British, then, after shifting allegiances, by the Germans.

The city is still surrounded by ghastly crumbling apartment buildings built by the Communists. There is a plan to demolish these but it's going to take years. In the older parts of the city there are hundreds of beautiful old houses, mostly in terrible condition. There's a search on now for the original owners, all of whom were tipped out into the streets by the regime. A few that have been restored are magnificent.

Very cold. No snow in the city but the surrounding mountains are covered. Visited the 'studio' Avi Lerner has bought. It's an old factory of some sort. Immense. No effort has been made to restore it. Many of the windows are broken and pools of water are everywhere as the roof leaks. Outside there are piles of rubbish. I ask why, if labour is so cheap here, they don't get a team of men and clean the place up a bit? No one answers the question.

On the other side of the city there is another studio also owned by Avi Lerner. This one is smaller but in much the same condition. There is a large staff, mostly young girls, nearly all of whom chain smoke. One film is being shot on a set. I watch for a while. It's a kickboxing movie, no doubt intended for DVD, with a couple of American kickboxers in the main roles. The cameraman is an Australian, Ross Clarkson, who's been living in Bulgaria for some years. The studio is managed by an Israeli named David Varod. He asks if I'd like him to supply me with 'some girls'. At first I think he means as secretaries or production assistants. But he doesn't mean this. I decline.

Spent one day travelling through mountains. Nearly all of *The Contract* is set in a forest, so it shouldn't be too difficult filming it here. Problem now is that there is so much snow, a lot of the roads are impassable. And it's hard to decide on locations which are going to look so different in the summer. Still, we found a good stretch of road with a slope down to a river that will be fine for the big scene of the car hijack.

The Bulgarian production manager, Bobby Ranghelov, told me of doing a film here (*The Profession of Arms*) with Ermanno Olmi.* He used only amateur actors and had them improvise the dialogue. Film didn't work (I saw it on DVD), but Olmi bought a lottery ticket during the shooting and won 4 million euros.

Bob Misiorowski told me he once worked on a *Rambo* film with Stallone, in Israel. Halfway through Stallone said

---

* Italian director, best known for *Tree of Wooden Clogs* (1978).

he was sick of Israel and they were to pack up and leave. Cost millions, but they moved the production to Arizona. Incredible what these big stars can get away with. They can even break contracts being fairly sure they won't be sued as the producers don't want to alienate them. They might need them for a future project.

I am staying in the Grand Hotel, an elegant faux-1930s building. Last night as I walked to the lift a well-dressed man approached and said 'goodnight' and then added, 'Do you want some comfort?' I asked him what he meant. He repeated it, then, because of my blank look, added 'a girl'. This deluge of girls hasn't happened on any other movie. As I declined and went on up to my lonely room he no doubt wrote me off as gay.

24th February 2005

Found more locations than I thought we would, including an apartment building, a street that could stand-in for Washington D.C. and even a park that can be turned into a cemetery. The real cemeteries here are nothing like American ones, so Herbert Pinter is going to have to build one. 'No problem,' he said. Always the best thing to hear from production designers.

Went to Plovdiv, a few hours away from Sofia on one of the new expressways — second largest city. Beautiful old town, but with lots more restoration needed. Some superb houses and a vast Roman theatre, which was only found about 30 years ago after a landslide. Now they're using it again for plays.

Mark Egerton is here, working as first* on the Brian De Palma† film *The Black Dahlia*, for which a Los Angeles street and part of a suburban housing area have been built just outside Sofia. Mark was in Australia for some years and was my first on *Breaker Morant*, *The Fringe Dwellers* and a number of other films, before he went back to England to manage his father's pheasant shoot in Yorkshire! He tells me this hasn't worked out too well. He complains about the Labour government in Britain; says they are anti-country — the fox hunting ban is putting thousands out of work and there are restrictions on the pheasant shooting.

I don't think we'd have made *Breaker Morant* if Egerton hadn't been on the film. We were shooting in South Australia in terrible weather and on a very tight schedule. No matter what the problems he worked out a way to overcome them. When the roads were impassable to a location he arranged to take the entire crew, cast and equipment out to the location on horseback.

---

* First assistant director. Key figure on a film set — responsible for the smooth running of the production. Usually organises the schedule for each day's filming and is expected to ensure the director sticks to it.

† American director. His films include *Mission Impossible* (1996) and *The Untouchables* (1987).

A handsome man, tall and blond with bright blue eyes, Mark was sent to Australia around the age of 20 as the black sheep of a prominent family. His scholastic achievements were sub-standard and I suppose it was considered a low IQ would be less noticeable in the Colonies. In fact, it turned out that he wasn't stupid but merely dyslectic. After a few years as a jackeroo he somehow drifted into the film industry where his organisational skills and sheer charm quickly propelled him to be the most sought after first assistant. His daughter, who I remember as a child, is now 22, extremely glamorous and works as his second assistant director. He tells me he gets on with Brian De Palma but that De Palma is not particularly friendly with his crew, who are forbidden to speak to him. Evidently there have been a lot of problems with Avi Lerner's group and De Palma took the precaution of bringing his own line producer from Los Angeles. Exactly what I tried to do with Richard Rothschild. I'm sure De Palma would have a lot more clout than I do.

27th February 2005

Now in London to cast the supporting roles. All are meant to be American, so I can audition American actors working in London, or English actors who can do the accent. Actors seems to be much better at accents than they were even ten years ago. Maybe with pay TV everyone gets to hear various accents much more. Australian actors, especially the young ones, don't seem to have trouble with any accents at all. Bryan Brown is almost the only Australian actor who seems unable — or unwilling — to do any accent other than his own.

The casting director is Jeremy Zimmerman. He has a tiny office, crammed with staff (the usual bunch of pretty girls) on a top floor off Carnaby Street. Seems very amiable. Being an ex-actor will be an advantage. Actors should trust him and he'll be able to contact them easily.

Call from Rabineau to say that John Cusack wants the film pushed back a week* as another film of his is behind schedule. This 'other film' has not been mentioned before by Rabineau, who must've known about it. He's Cusack's agent. I assume they've been waiting until *The Contract* deal was signed before springing this one. There have been so many delays on this project I'm not too thrilled. Now I understand how many directors go for five years between films.

At least in London I have a vast choice of plays, musicals and opera. Saw a revival of an old (1960s) Terence Rattigan play, *Man and Boy*, with a wonderful cast headed by David Suchet. Not such a brilliant piece, but better than most contemporary plays. It's about a crooked financier on the run, who hides out with his estranged son in a sleazy part of New York.

---

* This turned out to be three weeks.

Andrew Lloyd-Webber's *The Woman in White*. Amazing production with digital projection; incredibly elaborate. I must use this technique in my next opera production. I still can't follow the plot of *Woman in White* — couldn't when I tried to read the novel* and couldn't follow the musical, which must've been simplified, too. The music is quite tedious; nothing like as inventive as L-W's early works. It really is an example of the audience going out whistling the sets. Lloyd-Webber has certainly written a couple of the greatest musicals ever but has never found a lyricist to match Tim Rice. A shame they split up. Clive James could probably write lyrics as inventive as Rice's. I can't imagine why Lloyd-Webber hasn't contacted him. Probably hasn't heard any of the albums with Pete Atkin singing Clive's lyrics.

Lunch with Jeffrey Archer and Philip Bacon.† JA still amazed we haven't been able to cast and/or finance his Mallory script. The story of this disastrous Everest expedition of 1923 is SO exciting and the script so accomplished that it's difficult to see why it's aroused no interest, despite the enthusiasm of Richard Zanuck. I know I shouldn't be surprised. All too often it's the totally conventional scripts/stories that find backing. I realise the financiers want to, have to, make money from

---

* By Wilkie Collins and first published in 1860. Said to be the 'first mystery novel'. It certainly mystified me.

† Australian art dealer.

their investments and so much material they reject has an 'art house' appeal. But not everything. The Mallory story seems to me to be the basis of an enormously popular film. Jeffrey Archer is hardly an esoteric writer. His numerous novels are scorned by critics but immensely popular worldwide. For the new one, coming out at Christmas, he's been paid a $6 million advance.

Zanuck was confident that Jude Law would be interested in playing Mallory. Not the case. Ewan McGregor turned it down, too.

1st March 2005

Casting for *The Contract* going well. It's usually not too difficult to fill all the minor roles with good actors. They don't earn the money of the big stars, by a long chalk, and are willing to take on just about anything. The script of *The Contract* will be a test of their latitude.

A small camera is set up in a freezing room in Soho. The actors are given 'sides' — just a scene or two from the film, which they act out with someone standing beside the camera. This person is not seen but delivers the feed lines. In this case Jeremy Zimmerman gets his young son to do the off-camera reading. This boy would be well advised not to take up acting as a profession. It's almost insulting to have to put all these accomplished people down on tape, but everyone has to be approved at Avi's headquarters in Los Angeles, so there's no alternative. Not unreasonable, I suppose. They're paying money and want to see who they're getting. Quite a few of the actors coming in to read are Australians. Two of them, Jonathan Hyde and William Tapley, would be fine for substantial roles.

I realise, as if I didn't know already, that the dialogue still needs a lot of work. Despite J.D. Zeik's numerous rewrites, the characters still sound much the same and the clichés are abundant.

Back in my Bloomsbury flat (now free of tenants) I pour a large bourbon and watch Christian Duguay's *Screamers** again. Easily the best sci-fi film I've seen. A good story about a group abandoned on a distant planet where a mechanical enemy keeps evolving into different shapes and attacking them. Very frightening. Unusually among sci-fi stories, this one has an interesting group of characters and the dialogue is sharp. Hammers home to me that something has to be done about *The Contract*. Interesting that no one seems to be worried except me, probably because no one in the production company other than Boaz Davidson has read the script.

---

* Made in Quebec in 1995, and based on the short story written by Philip K. Dick, *Second Variety*. Among Christian Duguay's other films is an outstanding TV film, *Hitler, the Rise of Evil* (2003).

With Tommy Lee Jones — filming *Double Jeopardy*.

3rd March 2005

New York. Working yet again on the script with J.D. Zeik. Very tiring. Having heard so many actors trying to make the dialogue come alive and usually failing I'm intensely aware I'll be far better off with some decent lines than having to set the actors an impossible task. J.D. is agreeable about all my suggested alterations, probably too agreeable. He rapidly changes and adds scenes but are they any better? Or substantially different? On *Double Jeopardy* (which also had a dialogue problem), Tommy Lee Jones said to me one day, 'You're very lucky I'm in this film.' 'Why is that?' I asked. 'Who else,' he said, 'could make all this nonsense sound convincing.'

Barry Humphries is performing in New York. Picked him up at the end of his show and went to supper. He looks tired but OK. Just turned 70. Not bad to be a Broadway star at that age. All the material he was being urged to delete, by his New York advisors, has proved to be wildly popular and universally favourably commented on by the critics. I asked him if the 'advisors' had ever admitted their mistake. Of course not.

4th March 2005

A lot of phone calls about the film. They were originally insisting on Dante Spinotti as cameraman. I couldn't object as I know how talented he is and have already worked with him on *Crimes of the Heart* and my section of *Aria*. Now it seems Dante is too expensive. His normal fee is around US$25,000 per week (phew) and I'm told they've offered $10,000. If they can't compromise I suggested they contact Peter James, who is every bit as talented, though I doubt if he'd accept the $10,000 either.

Adam and his new girlfriend, Vanessa, arrived from Boston. She's from Colombia; speaks perfect English. She is quiet, so far at any rate. She and Adam keep chatting away in Spanish so I've no idea what they're talking about.

Vincent De Ville *still* insists he has the money for the Semmelweiss film. This is getting tedious. Rabineau says he doesn't have a penny. Hard to work these things out. I'm fairly sure Rabineau is right. If Vincent really had the money, as he says, we'd be making the film by now. We'd have started it long ago. Years ago, in fact.

Lunch with Barry Humphries, Adam and Vanessa and my old friend John Simon, an ex-Harvard professor, who has been a critic for years — of film, theatre and music. Always being accused of being overcritical and destructive, though this seems absurd to me. He has immense enthusiasm for many things, it's just that when he tears into something his turn of phrase is devastating. In a TV debate with Gore Vidal, Vidal dismissed some viewpoint of John's on the basis that English isn't John's first language (he was born in Croatia of Hungarian parents).

'Quite right,' said John, in his slightly accented (but still perfect) English, 'it's my fifth.'

With John Simon went to a preview of an excellent play, *Moonlight and Magnolias*, by Ron Hutchinson. About the stalled production three weeks into the shooting of *Gone With the Wind*. Evidently Louis B. Mayer stopped production, unhappy with the progress of the shoot, with the script and with the director, George Cukor. He threatened to cancel the film entirely and gave producer David Selznick a week in which to solve the problems. The play is set entirely in Selznick's office (meticulously recreated), where Selznick and the replacement director, Victor Fleming, try to convince an unwilling writer, Ben Hecht, to do a rapid rewrite. An added problem is that Hecht has never read the novel so has to write while the story is acted out to him by Selznick and Fleming. Very funny and perceptive. At one point Selznick goes on and on about how they have to have crushed ice in glasses as Southerners at that time didn't have ice cubes. I'm sure he was this fanatical — at the same time he thought nothing of shooting the movie on sets that were basically theatrical (nothing was filmed on location) and using actors who made no attempt at a Southern accent.*

---

* Looking at the film again on DVD, Vivien Leigh DID attempt a Southern accent, somewhat erratically. Clark Gable was just his usual self, but is well cast and his underplaying means the performance is engaging today — over 60 years later. Leslie Howard is far too old for his role and sounds totally English. He appears to have wandered in from another movie.

A clever touch before the beginning of the play —
as the audience takes their seats — screen tests from
Gone with the Wind are projected. At least a dozen
actresses trying for the role of Scarlett O'Hara,
including Bette Davis and Paulette Goddard. The play
ends with Ben Hecht and Victor Fleming both refusing
to take a percentage of the film in lieu of salary.
Immediately after the last line, 'I know a turkey when
I see one', the opening of the movie hits the screen
with its famous theme (stolen by Max Steiner from
Beethoven's Waldstein sonata) and its titles blowing
across right to left.

5th March 2005

Saw Jessica Lange in *The Glass Menagerie*. This is a
celebrated play, but there is something insipid about this
production. A new play, *Brooklyn Boy* by Donald Margulies,
is much more affecting though the writing isn't really up
to the level of the Tennessee Williams. A Jewish boy from
Brooklyn, who has made it big in Hollywood, returns
home to visit his dying father. A lot of the issues raised
(filial relationships, selling out to the movies, etc) have
been dealt with before, but everything seemed to me to
ring true. At the end of the play, after the curtain calls, an
old Jewish lady sitting in the next seat turned to me and
said, 'Wasn't that wonderful?' Impossible not to agree.

6th March 2005

In LA now. Dinner with John Cusack, who I'd only met once before. Very tall. He must be at least 6 foot 2 and powerfully built. Most leading men are relatively short; no idea why — Tom Cruise, Mel Gibson, Robert Redford. It's hard to tell on screen how tall actors really are. I'd always assumed that James Mason was average height, and was amazed, when I met him, to see he was considerably taller than me — 6 foot. Julie Christie I'd always thought was a tall woman, but she must only be around 5 foot 1.

I discuss *The Contract* with John, trying not to give away the fact I'm still very unhappy with the script, though I gather he isn't all that enamoured of it either; he must've been swayed by Avi's financial offer and, perhaps, the idea of working with me. I assure him we're still rewriting and that I'll get a new draft to him . . . Anyway, he seems quite pleasant, very bright, and I've seen him in enough films to know he is a versatile actor. I'm less worried now about his age. He's 40, so it's not implausible he could have a son of 13. I thought he was younger. It's just that I'm getting so old anyone under 50 looks very young.

7th March 2005

I go to one of the few art-house theatres in LA to see *Downfall*, about Hitler's last days in the bunker. Very compelling with Bruno Ganz easily the most convincing Hitler I've seen on screen — and there have been a hell of a lot of them. (Alec Guinness even played him (badly) in one film.*) All the scenes in the bunker and those of the Russian army closing in on the city are staged with total realism. Casting is meticulous throughout, with all the actors strongly resembling those they're portraying. Very few people in the theatre. Not surprising, this is a place where all the emphasis is on commercial movies. Everyone goes to see the latest studio films, even if they loathe them, as they have to stay up to date on story trends and the up-and-coming stars.

This theatre on Wilshire is where *Breaker Morant* opened in 1982. There was almost no audience at all. It ran only three days!

Met with Evzen Kolar. He still has nothing going. His script about the Shakespeare forgers and his one about Handel writing his *Messiah* have aroused no interest at all. Both need extensive rewriting, but no one has come forward with the finance to do this. A shame. Both would make excellent films. He gives me a DVD of a low-budget feature he produced on the Isle of Man where some bizarre tax benefit scheme operates. It's opening in a week or so in a limited release.

Avi's office has still not resolved the cameraman for *The Contract*. Peter James quoted much the same as Dante

---

* *Hitler, the Last Ten Days*, directed by Ennio De Concini in 1973.

Spinotti, so they've gone back to Spinotti. Josh Maurer*
called. He's arranging a meeting with network execs re a
TV mini-series of *Papillon*. Josh assures me it's not a
remake of the old movie, but is taken from both books
written by Henri Charrière, about his experiences on
Devil's Island. A lot of doubt has been cast on the
authenticity. There have been allegations Charrière wasn't
on Devil's Island at all, as he claimed, but got his stories
from ex-prisoners he met in France.

Saw Pieter Kroonenburg who still doesn't have a
director for his Chet Baker film. With a bit of luck he
won't get one and I'll be able to do it after *The Contract*.

Evening. Watched Evzen Kolar's film, *The Boys from
County Clare*. It's pleasant enough — all about a music
competition in Ireland — though it has some huge holes
in the plot. Problem is it's just not what they call 'high
concept'† enough to attract an audience. At least, I don't
think so. I could be wrong. I've been to a number of
previews, confidently predicted success or failure and the
opposite proved to be the case. After the preview of *As
Good as it Gets* I assured my friends it would be a financial

* Executive producer on *Pancho Villa*. One of the rare producers with a flair
for finding exciting stories. Uncommonly though, he does all his own
research. He presented me with hundreds of pages of material and numerous
photographs for *Pancho Villa*.

† A fashionable phrase at the moment in LA. It usually means some sort of
audience appeal rather than straight storytelling, eg the story could be told
backwards, there could be some technical gimmick or some promotable
publicity angle.

disaster. It made a fortune and won Helen Hunt an Academy Award.

9th March 2005

Meeting with Josh Hartnett in the bar of hotel on Beverly. Tall and impossibly handsome, he is dressed in clothes that could have been taken off a derelict. A woollen cap pulled low over his forehead further makes him resemble one of those people seen on TV in black and white staccato replays of convenience-store robberies. I assume that this disguise is to put predatory young women off the trail.

Josh is enthusiastic about the idea of a film about Chet Baker. Not a man with a light touch, he regales me for an hour or more with a monologue extolling his total dedication as an actor and his intention to make a wonderful film. The implication seems to be that no one else involved in the project shares his seriousness of purpose.

The meeting with Josh ranks fairly high in my list of tortured actor encounters. The worst was probably my lunch with Harrison Ford, in which he failed to say even one word but just made guttural ape-like noises. Coming a close second was my meeting with Jack Palance at a film festival. Seeing him standing alone with a glass in his hand, I went up to him, introduced myself and then congratulated him on some recent film of his. He snorted at me and strode away.

10th March 2005

More auditions for *The Contract* with the LA casting director. Her assistant, a voluptuous young woman, is wearing nothing under her thin cotton see-through dress.

I am looking mainly for the two women in the *The Contract*. One is an older (forties) White House exec, the other a young hiker. All of the girls who come in read very well — no mean feat considering the frightful dialogue. I'm told most of them are in considerable demand and a decision will have to be made quickly or we'll lose them. A young African–American girl seems to be ideal for the hiker.

I suggest that Alice Krige* might be ideal for the White House exec. The casting director is hostile to the idea for no clearly expressed reason. She resists the idea of asking Alice to come in for a meeting.† Casting directors play favourites, which is often very annoying as they can easily sabotage a director's suggestions for roles. Some (most?) are wildly eccentric — when I was casting *Tender Mercies* in New York, in 1981, the casting director (a woman; I've erased her name) objected violently when I chose a young

---

* South African-born actress. Best known for *Chariots of Fire* (1981) and *Barfly* (1987).

† I persisted with Alice. Met her in London a few months later and cast her in the role.

actor named Lenny van Dohlen to play the leader of the country and western band. Her objection was based on the fact that Lenny was one of the first people I'd seen. This hardly seemed to disqualify him, I objected, as he appeared to be ideal for the part. I wasn't aware of being under an obligation to cast only the actors who appeared at the tail end of the session. Furious, she resigned the job on the spot and stormed out. Unluckily, I ran into her that night inside the Lincoln Center, where I'd gone to see an opera. She continued her tirade from earlier in the day at the top of her voice, much to the bewilderment of the opera patrons who must've been under the impression that I'd done something dreadful.

11th March 2005

Vincent De Ville came around to the hotel with two men he introduced as the money raisers for *Fever*. As he's been telling me for two years that he has the finance I can't see why these people are needed. Neither inspire confidence in any event. Both seem to be distinctly low rent. They even dress like con men. One of them has been in Australia and was connected with a film that starred Jack Thompson. He urged me to call Jack for a personal recommendation.

Met with four young actresses for roles in *The Contract*. These are all recommendations from Randy Emmett. All are pretty but bimbos. And the key role we're looking for is a high-powered Washington White House executive! LA is full of these girls; I think most of them end up as the girlfriends of studio executives or friends of studio executives. The ones who make it as actresses usually seem to be bright, not just pretty. I remember a few years ago commenting to a successful producer that his glamorous girlfriend didn't seem to be too smart (this was after a conversation in which it was revealed she'd never heard of World War II). 'No,' he agreed, 'but she's got a great tush.'

I receive a message from the production office saying the African–American actress is not acceptable to play the hiker. I object, saying that her skin colour is not an issue — she's just the most suitable choice for the role. I'm then told that it's 'hard to sell films around the world with black actors'. Could this possibly be true? In 2005!! And what about the fact that Morgan Freeman is playing the leading role? My objections are overruled. I have to find a white girl for the part.

13th March 2005

Back in Australia. Slept nearly all the way. Saw Mike Nichols' movie, *Closer*, from the Patrick Marber play. Astonishingly frank dialogue. Amazing to hear Julia Roberts discussing sucking cocks and men coming in her mouth! Imagine my parents watching this! Yet no one turns a hair today.

Called Jack Thompson about Vincent De Ville's money sources. Jack tells me that they were disastrous and caused chaos on the movie. Normally very easy going and generous in his assessment of everyone, Jack now put the knife in with vehemence. Interesting that the two guys in question were so insistent I phone Jack. They obviously had no idea of how they were perceived.

15th March 2005

Interesting meeting with the scientist Tim Flannery at Beyond to discuss the Discovery Channel documentary about Australia, although I'm still not sure to what extent I will be able to incorporate his themes.

Saw *The Square Ring** on DVD — an Ealing boxing film with an ensemble cast that I remember seeing on the lower half of a double bill at the Parramatta Astra in 1953. I was very impressed by its realism at the time. It was one of those films that made me want to be a film director. The film stands up remarkably well; it's quite a fluid adaptation of a stage play by the Australian writer Ralph Peterson. All the actors are dead now, except for Joan

---

* Directed by Basil Dearden (1953).

Collins. Ronald Lewis committed suicide and George
Rose was murdered in Jamaica. Jack Warner went bonkers
in his old age and wandered the streets imagining he was
really 'Dixon of Dock Green' — the policeman he played
in a famous TV series.

20th March 2005

Two days on Gold Coast filming a huge surf carnival
for the Discovery Channel documentary. These are a
staple of documentaries about Australia, in fact it's hard
to think of one that doesn't have a surf carnival
sequence.

Dinner with Ingo Petzke — German professor of
film I met years ago in Wurzburg, Germany, where he
showed about a dozen of my films. He's now teaching in
the film department at Bond University. He wrote a
biography of Phil Noyce and wants to do one of me,
though it means 100 hours of interviews. I can't face
this and said no.

A call from Aurelio De Laurentiis, nephew of Dino,
asking if I've read a recently published Italian thriller,
I Kill, written by the actor Giorgio Faletti, as he believes
it will make an excellent film. It's not yet published in
English, but he's had a translation done and will Fedex it
to me.

23rd March 2005

In Coober Pedy, shooting part of the documentary (opal mining) for Beyond/Discovery. Desert town, pretty grim, though locals are friendly enough. About 1000 Aborigines, out of a population of 3000, who are a sorry lot for the most part. Dozens of them sit around in the shade all day, looking terrible. The children are better, often very beautiful. Healthy and alert. Horrible dinner at a Greek restaurant, allegedly barramundi. Quite inedible. I told the owner this in response to her question and she countered by pointing to a large group of people at another table who thought the meal 'wonderful'.

We spend a couple of days crawling around opal mines and interviewing some of the miners. A few have stories of fabulous 'strikes' (a couple even have vast chunks of opal to prove it), but most tell tales of endless digging in 40-plus degree C temperatures and finding virtually nothing. I have the feeling many of them find more opal than they admit to, but don't want this advertised on TV because of possible visits from the tax office.

We are told to be careful walking around as there are abandoned diggings everywhere. These consist of unmarked holes in the ground, often partially obscured by scrub, which drop straight down for hundreds of feet. We are repeatedly told a story, with relish, of the photographer accompanying a government minister who took a few steps back for a better angle and immediately plummeted to his death.

We plan to photograph a small barren range of hills, but are told this is Aboriginal 'sacred ground' and can't be photographed. At the local tourist office, an Aboriginal woman tells us to go ahead with our photography, but to avoid one particular hill that she marks for us on a map.

Message from Rich Cowan.* He has been preparing a film with a budget of $120 million but the studio has suddenly pulled the plug. So — can he work on *The Contract*? (He had told me he wouldn't be available because of the other film. Huge relief. I'm sure *The Contract* won't be easy to organise and I wasn't looking forward to trying to find a replacement.)

28th March 2005

Now at William Creek, where we're staying while filming at Anna Creek station. Town consists of two small ramshackle hotels. My room isn't too bad; at least there is an air conditioner. Incredibly noisy, but who cares. This is the cool season but it's around 40 degrees C during the day.

---

*   A Canadian. My first assistant on a number of films.

Vincent Perez (actor), Rich Cowan (first assistant director) and me all looking at a video playback of an action scene for *Bride of the Wind*. (Photograph by Harold Staudach)

I'm told there are more kangaroos than people in Australia but find this impossible to believe. I haven't seen one on this trip, even at dawn or dusk, which is when they're usually around.

I ask if I can make a phone call from the hotel. I am shown a phone on the bar and told it works only with a phone card. I then offer to buy one and am told 'we don't sell them'. It evidently hasn't occurred to the hotel owners that it might be a good idea to do so. Naturally, there is nowhere else here to buy one. I am informed I can get one in Coober Pedy, 120 km away.

A hellishly hot day filming a cattle round up (done on motorbikes). We begin at 4.15 am. Heat is frightful though the locals think it's 'cool' and the millions of flies 'aren't too bad'. Randall, the station manager, tells me that a husband and wife doctor team were on a trip to Lake Eyre last year when their four-wheel drive bogged in the sand. They decided to walk the 60 km back to the station. After 20 km they had an argument about what to do. He walked back to the car and she walked on. She died some kilometres further on, not realising that the small embankments a few hundred metres from the road were dams with water. He made it back to the car and was rescued the next day.

We shoot an interview with a pretty but quite unremarkable girl of 17 who is working as a jillaroo on the station. I fear the producers are more interested in her than Fiona Wood, the doctor who has developed the new treatment for burns.

29th March 2005

Another 4.30 am start to shoot a cattle drive at dawn. Then we move to film the two boys, sons of the station manager, doing lessons via internet, but the computer doesn't work. Evidently it's hardly worked all year, but no one seems to mind.

Back at the 'hotel', the wife of the owner tells me that July and August are the busy months, when lots of 'grey nomads' visit — that is, retired people who just buy a caravan and travel for the rest of their lives around Australia.

4th April 2005

Sydney. Travelled a full day to get back from William Creek. First plane, a small one, had to stop at Roxby Downs and refuel as it didn't have enough fuel to fly direct to Adelaide — because of the heat, evidently.

The novel, *I Kill*, has arrived from Italy. Two immense hardbound volumes. It must be as long as *Gone With the Wind*. Still, if I sit down and just read them it should only take a couple of days. I read the whole of *Les Miserables* in about three days and made extensive notes on it when there was talk of filming the musical. That, of course, all came to nothing.

Cordelia seems to be having a tough time filming in Vietnam.* They're in a beautiful but remote area and are disorganised. There is no first assistant and the director, inexperienced, just decides what to shoot — on whim, it seems. The interpreter has despaired and quit, leaving C with no one to talk to. The leading lady speaks some English but is married to the director.

5th April 2005

I suggest we film Ross Edwards at a concert in Melbourne, where the orchestra is performing a new piece of his. But permission is refused to shoot in the concert hall, so we can only shoot the rehearsal. Tricky talking the Discovery people into this as they don't seem too keen to film him at all.

7th April 2005

Finish reading *I Kill*. A thriller, set in Monte Carlo, rather in the vein of the Hannibal Lecter books. This time a mysterious murderer is bumping people off around the port area. Quite involved, with a hell of a lot of murders, two detectives (one an American), a radio DJ

---

* She is photographing a feature film there, *The Story of Apa*.

and a computer expert. May make an effective film, though the story would need a lot of reshaping.

11th April 2005

We film Riley Lee, soloist in the Ross Edwards piece (on a shakuhachi — a kind of Japanese flute), in Melbourne, then I go to Richmond, Tasmania, to do an interview with Chris Koch. This has to be sent to Washington (Discovery head office) to be approved before we can shoot the interview for real. Bit elaborate. A nuisance having to get permission, from someone in the USA, to film all these bits and pieces. Very frustrating, too, to have no direct contact with these controllers. Have they read the detailed outline I wrote for the documentary? Did they approve it? Even in part?

I suggested that it would make an interesting sequence to cover the search for the Tasmanian tiger. The animal has been extinct since the late 1930s but there have been many alleged sightings, none of them too convincing. All the same, there are numerous groups in Tasmania dedicated to combing the forests in search of the animal — and they're now spurred on by a reward of over $1 million for an authenticated sighting. My suggestion met with a tepid response, though I pointed out we could include old footage of the tigers and tie it in with the theme of conservation. My research revealed a fascinating story. Some people in Tasmania were aware that the animal — unique in the world — was in decline, through hunting, from as early as the 1890s. Groups lobbied in the State Parliament to have it protected. Finally, an Act was passed in 1943, seven years after the death of the last tiger.

Still no news from Avi's office re Spinotti vis-à-vis Peter James to photograph *The Contract*. I think they're doing a deal with Mark Warner to edit the film.*

Avi Lerner's production company offered Rich Cowan a modest fee for six weeks preparation of *The Contract*. He said he wanted eight weeks, so they came back and offered the same fee for eight weeks. Clever. He was so stunned, he accepted.

A wonderful Korean film on TV, *Musa* (*The Warrior*).† Terrific design and costumes, and easily the best staged fights I've seen. Great to see an Asian film where they're not running up walls and skipping across lakes and treetops. The fights in this film are realistic, there is a fascinating group of characters and the dialogue, even in subtitles, is often very touching. A gripping story, set in the 14th century, of a group of Koreans on a mission to China who are caught in the middle of a local power struggle and have to fight their way back to Korea, while being pursued

---

* Mark Warner edited *Driving Miss Daisy*, *Double Jeopardy* and *And Starring Pancho Villa as Himself*.

† Written and directed by Sung-su Kim (2001).

by a bunch of fierce Mongol warriors. A sophisticated script. Even the Mongols, despite all their ferocity, are portrayed with sympathy. In one scene, they are sitting around a campfire complaining about the loss of Genghis Khan and the grand old days of the empire. The love affair between the eponymous Warrior (Woo-sung Jung) and the captive Chinese princess (Ziyi Zhang) is intensely moving. His death, protecting her, must be one of the greatest moments in all of cinema.

13th April 2005

An afternoon filming an AFL game in Sydney, again for the documentary. The Swans lost. Played very badly. All so morose at the end of the game there was no point in interviewing the coach, Paul Roos, who appeared to be suicidal. Adam Goodes, the gifted Aboriginal player, did a desultory piece. We should film them again after a win. This footage will be useless.

21st April 2005

Bucharest, Romania. I have been invited here as President of the Jury at a film festival. Was met by the festival director, Dana Dimitriu, a tall, strident woman in her forties with what looks to me like a fake suntan, and, maybe, with failed lip implants. All lip implants fail. They produce the odd effect of having speech appear to be out of synch, like a movie where the soundtrack has slipped.

Dana is a terrible driver (common in Romania). We were stopped by the police after nearly hitting an old woman at a crossing. Dana also wears no seat belt. She tells me she never wears one. Doesn't even put it on when we drive off, even though the policeman is watching. Nearer the city we are stopped again for speeding.

Dinner with her and another young woman, also a festival organiser. Both tell me their parents' houses were taken by the Communists in the 1940s and have never been given back. Evidently all the middle-class people were thrown out of their homes, which were then handed over to 'workers' or party officials. (Dana says that the party members arrived at her parents' house and said, 'You have 20 minutes. You can take with you whatever you can pack in that time.') Now the houses can be claimed back, but many of the original owners are dead, don't have papers to prove ownership (Communists gave no compensation and no receipts) or are too old to be bothered. There are thousands of more or less derelict houses all over the city. A few are restored, some turned into restaurants, etc, but most still need attention.

The film festival opening is tonight, but last night the opening film had not arrived and the French Institute, who were throwing the opening night party, have decided to cancel. Interesting to see what happens.

We drove past Ceausescu's vast palace — the second biggest building in the world (the Pentagon is the biggest) but still unfinished. Evidently he demolished some of the most beautiful parts of the city to build it. Now they don't know what to do with it.

22nd April 2005

A good film by Antonia Bird, *The Hamburg Cell*, about the group who did the September 11 tragedy. A fascinating study of a group of fanatics, good characterisations and not hysterical. Well acted by an unknown Arab cast. Afternoon film was a 1960s type underground movie from Kiev, *Guidebook*. Awful. Walked out.

The opening night film, *Promised Land*, still hasn't arrived. The director, Amos Gitai, has — from LA — and he isn't happy. We go to dinner with him. He is understandably fairly surly. Everyone is fed up with him anyway. Evidently he refused to stay in the hotel where the rest of the festival guests (including me) are staying as it's 'only 3 star'. Insisted he was taken to a 5-star hotel.

A Romanian director at the dinner has a conversation with him about politics. Gitai (an Israeli) is left wing and announces that the experience of Communism in Eastern Europe 'wasn't representative' of Communism and could be discounted. The Romanian asks if he thought the same was true of Nazism. Would he say the experience of countries and people under the Nazis was 'not representative'?

25th April 2005

Toured Ceausescu's palace. Parquet floors, marble columns, vast carpets and curtains. One reception room is bigger than a football field. A third of the city was demolished so it could be built. Astonishing. Even more astonishing is how he managed to hold on to power for so long when he was clearly beggaring the country while spending everything on himself. I asked the tour guide — yet another beautiful girl — what the palace is used for now. 'Weddings and parties,' she replies.

We give 'best film' to a charming Japanese film consisting of three love stories — all between a Japanese boy or girl and a Chinese boy or girl, who didn't speak the other's language very well. Can't imagine why I ever thought that the Japanese had no sense of humour.

Best director to Antonia Bird for *Hamburg Cell*.

Dana suddenly announced an award to the strange Romanian film, which I found pretentious and incomprehensible. This award came as a surprise to the jury! No explanation is offered. I suppose it was politically advisable to hand out at least one award to a Romanian film. The director made a short acceptance speech in perfect English. He is a very good-looking actor/director, a dead ringer for Colin Firth.

26th April 2005

Dana took me to the airport. Another frightening drive in her paper-stream car. She was furious with the two guests from Kiev — a young director who dressed like a pirate and spent his days wandering around the city, plus his attractive young production assistant(?), who spoke excellent English. Evidently they ran up a room-service bill of hundreds of dollars. Mostly on vodka.

27th April 2005

In London. More casting sessions for *The Contract*. Still have to find a young woman to play the hiker, as the black girl isn't acceptable(!).

Saw an Alan Bennett play, *The History Boys*, on its last night. Bennett took a curtain call. Novel structure and well played with interesting observations about history and the way it's recounted. I'm getting a bit tired of these Bennett school-obsessed pieces. Richard Griffiths gives a charismatic performance as one of the teachers, though he'd be well advised to lose 100 pounds or so. I should put him in touch with my personal trainer.

28th April 2005

Meetings. First with Clive James. Met at his apartment. Beautifully furnished, with books lining every wall and an interesting collection of pictures, many of literary figures. The place is always immaculate. No piles of papers as in my study. Even his work desk is neat. He has a computer but doesn't use it to write. Everything is done in pencil in exercise books. He's extraordinarily industrious. Must've had a couple of dozen books published — including memoirs, novels, criticism and poetry.

He's finishing two books. Just had a poem in *The Spectator*, which is a eulogy to his wife, Prue. I'm always a little suspicious of friends who trumpet their uxoriousness.

Lunch with Laurence Myers* and writer Tom Kinninmore to discuss their script set in East Africa. Deals with a group of British builders who go to a holiday resort then find the local kids have no school. They get together and build one. A neat story and true. Basically, at least. I think the script still needs a lot of work. I advise eliminating the subplot where the main character has a delinquent stepson in England. Why not take this boy with him to Africa and show a change in his personality and attitudes when he's confronted with real deprivation? Laurence Myers thinks they can find the

---

* Well-known producer, mainly of West End theatre.

money IF there are a couple of 'names' in the cast. The old problem. Every project chasing the same names.

Met with Bill Gavin to discuss, once again, *Master Class* — from the play about Stalin tormenting Shostakovich and Prokofiev. He thinks Michael Gambon still might play Stalin — a role no one seems to want. God knows why not. Another problem is that the man who owns the rights is difficult to deal with and inclined to reject actors who would in fact be ideal for the roles. Doubt if Gavin is doing well these days, despite his success with *Whale Rider*. He looks old (I guess I do, too) and has an office about the size of a phone booth. At least he's crammed in there with a gorgeous Brazilian secretary.

Then met with producer Fred Mueller at the Groucho Club to discuss the Rachmaninoff project. Interesting project. He thinks the script will be ready at the end of June and finance is possible, partially from Russia. Again, it's all about casting. I suggest Vincent Perez,* who looks like Rachmaninoff and is a first-class actor. I sense a lack of enthusiasm for Perez, probably because the finance won't enthuse over him.

We chat briefly with a visiting American producer. 'Who is this Rachmaninoff?' she asks. I don't think we're going to get a lot of help there. I don't expect everyone to have heard of Rachmaninoff, but how could a film producer with a college education possibly have reached middle age and not

---

* Handsome bi-lingual French actor.

be aware that Sergei Rachmaninoff was a major 20th-century composer and one of its most celebrated pianists? Classical music seems to be a closed book to film producers and financiers. A few years ago when I was pushing a script (*Bride of the Wind*) about Gustav and Alma Mahler around Los Angeles, I was asked, in reference to Mahler, 'Why would you want to make a film about a nonentity?'

1st May 2005

In Paris to meet with Michel Suriez, a French stunt arranger who has done brilliant work on *Bon Voyage* and *Fanfan La Tulipe*, about *The Contract*. I think a deal has already been done for *The Contract* with the Canadian, Michael Scherer, but probably worth meeting Michel anyway. He's around 40, speaks good English, personable.

Spend a day walking around the city. I look through the small galleries on the left bank and buy a delightful 1920s pastel drawing by Louis Legrand (1854–1951). Saw a Bruce Willis film, *Hostage*, which is totally ridiculous. The situation, where three young tough guys are holding a family hostage in their own house, is so overstated it's quite comical. The ending turns into a horror film, with a nonsensical final shoot-out between Willis and a bunch of masked baddies. The story makes *The Contract* seem positively logical. Even Willis' intense performance doesn't help make it credible. Could this film make money?

Filming a scene for *Bride of the Wind*. Jonathan Price as Gustav Mahler.
(Photograph by Harold Staudach)

I'll suggest to Boaz Davidson at NuImage that we pay
Tim Prager for a week's work revising *The Contract* script.
Without this it's going to be a hell of a job directing.

4th May 2005

Writing this flying from Spokane, Washington, to Los
Angeles. Spent a day in Spokane looking for locations.
We're to shoot there a couple of days for some American
authenticity — the rest of the film is being shot in Bulgaria.
Spokane is a super-clean city, quite small, with the totally
dead centre so characteristic of American cities — all the
business has gone to shopping malls in the suburbs. The
centre has one empty storefront after another. Stayed in a
well-restored hotel built in 1914 (The Davenport) — can't
imagine who comes to stay as it's so vast. Comfortable beds,
but breakfast served cold. How do they do this with eggs?
    With Herbert Pinter and Bobby Ranghelov, plus Rich
Cowan (that is, Australian designer, Bulgarian production
manager, Canadian first assistant) we drive around
suburban areas until I spot a modest house that seems
ideal for the exterior of John Cusack's house. (He's playing
a gym teacher so it can't be too fancy.) The interior is to
be built in Sofia. We knock on the door and are greeted
by a friendly old guy who lives here alone. He is quite
thrilled to have a film crew visiting and rapidly agrees to
photographs and measurements being taken. I look around

his living room. Lots of family photos. I think his wife has died and his children grown up and gone away.

Our local liaison guy takes us to a rocky area overlooking the city. This will be fine for some establishing shots of the town. After that, it'll be a straight cut to the material shot halfway around the world.

Finished reading Simon Gray's *The Smoking Diaries*. Frightfully dull, despite the critical endorsement on the back of it as 'sublimely absurd'.

Boaz Davidson approves Tim Prager doing a rewrite on the script. I think he must've picked up the desperate tone in my voice. I'm sorry it hasn't worked out with J.D. Zeik. He's bright and agreeable, which is why I think I've believed for so long that the script was going to make sense at last. I also think he's talented. I read a couple of his original scripts and they're well done. I think the difference is that commissioned rewrite jobs just don't inspire.

6th May 2005

Tim Prager has read the script of *The Contract*. His opening comment to me is, 'I can't believe they're going to finance this.' He's right. Why on earth did I take on this one? I hated it at the beginning. I guess it was only because none of the projects I believed in have found finance. And I know I like to keep shooting. Hate being inactive.

Certainly I've been relentlessly steered toward this by my
agent at William Morris, but I can't really blame him.
There was plenty of time for me to pull out. I always
thought the Wilberforce film would go ahead, as it now
has, even though the agent said it was unlikely. No point
in complaining. I can't really blame anyone else for my
bad decisions. I'll just have to do the best job I can on *The
Contract*.

Tim agrees with me that the current running time of
the script is only around 75 minutes. 'This,' he says, 'is
because it doesn't have a plot.' True. Once the father, son
and grandfather (a character Tim thinks should be
eliminated) meet the escaped criminal (Morgan Freeman)
in the forest, there is no complexity in the following chase.
It needs some double-crosses, some variations, more
character conflict. I hope he can come up with a few
ideas. We'll talk it over when I get to London.

On a whim I Google one of the actresses, Dawn Yanek,
that I met in LA. She seems to be some kind of sex
therapist, with magazine columns and a TV show advising
women about their sex lives!

12th May 2005

In London. Casting went OK in LA, as well as here.
Now, a list turns up from Avi Lerner of actors he wants
me to use. All the major roles! Most of them I don't know,

the ones I do are unsuitable. Why wouldn't he have given me this list before casting began, not when it's almost over?

Visit Tim Prager in his rather glamorous house in Fulham. He has a study on the top floor where he furtively smokes. We discuss various possibilities for adding some density to the plot of *The Contract*. He is going to remove the grandfather. In the first place, he points out, the grandfather has the longest scenes in the film — up until the point where he is killed casually and brutally by the bad guys. This would be so shattering to his son and grandson that it would affect their behaviour for all the subsequent scenes. Yet, in the present draft, they don't show all that much interest! Further, if the script is rewritten so that they do, which would be more plausible, then it will affect, adversely, their relationship with the chief bad guy, Morgan Freeman. So, grandfather will go. I have an idea that the actor cast to play him, Bill Smitrovich, might be happy to play the police chief instead — especially as that role will now be built up.

Rush to see *Kingdom of Heaven*, Ridley Scott's new film, just released. It's disappointing. Weakly scripted. No story at all and a number of risible dialogue scenes. Major actors — Jeremy Irons and David Thewlis — have little to do, they're practically extras, while the burden of the film is thrust onto an unconvincing Orlando Bloom. He has none of the authority and certainly none of the charisma that Russell Crowe brought to *Gladiator*. I sense that the released film is a cut-down version of a much longer movie. Ridley remains one of the greatest directors ever all the same. His visual flair is unparalleled. Just look at the visual design of *Blade Runner*, *Alien*, *The Duellists* or, for that matter, any of his other films.

On stage — Pinter's *The Birthday Party*. A wonderful play, funny and sinister. Some of the acting could've been more naturalistic. Pinter doesn't work if it's played any other way. I've often read articles describing Pinter's plays as surreal. They certainly deal with odd situations, but I find them totally believable. As a young actor in the provinces I'm sure Pinter encountered a lot of the events portrayed in his early plays, and I'll bet that his complicated love life has provided the basis of many of the others. It is also not true that his dialogue — with it's repetitions and pauses — is unrealistic. In fact, I think he has an uncanny ear for speech patterns. Every time I eavesdrop on Londoners talking, on the bus or on a train, it sounds like dialogue from a Pinter play.

Call from Pat Duggan insisting he has the money for *Curlow Creek*. He read me a letter from Bob Yari,* which Pat thinks is a promise of investment. It's no such thing; it's a standard Hollywood letter not really offering help but keeping options open — just in case we come up with a big star, I suppose.

---

* A major Hollywood independent. Produced the award-winning *Crash* (2004).

13th May 2OO5

Neil LaBute play, *In the Company of Men*, at the Donmar. A three hander, with a little less of the misogyny characteristic of this writer (a factor that would seem to mitigate against the barrage of critical praise for LaBute, but hasn't done so). The young woman in the play, an American actress named Megan Dodds, would be ideal for the girl hiker in *The Contract*. I'll ask Zimmerman to check her availability through her agent. Probably OK, as this play will have finished its run. Actors in Europe are usually quite relaxed about filming anywhere from Dublin to Bucharest, as they can always fly home for a weekend or on days off. Much harder to get them to go to Australia, where they're so far away from home they're stuck there for the shoot.

14th May 2OO5

In Cannes — as the guest of Aurelio De Laurentiis. Although the film festival is in full swing, Aurelio has arranged a room for me in The Carlton, the most prestigious hotel. This was impossible when I was here in 1980 with *Breaker Morant* — and it was in competition.

Aurelio is here with his staff and family — a good-looking son and daughter, plus a very elegant wife. All speak perfect English. The daughter must be 4 inches taller than Aurelio, is pretty but rather surly. Gives every indication of being totally bored. I suppose it isn't much fun for her sitting around listening to her dad discussing film projects with various strangers.

We talk about *I Kill* at some length. All agree there are too many murders. I suggest that Tim Prager might be a good writer for the script. He's written a ten-part cop series for the BBC, an original, so has experience with the genre. Aurelio keeps breaking into Italian to discuss the prospects of a football team he owns — in Naples, I think.

Evening. We all go to a superb fish restaurant a couple of miles from the centre of town. Getting into the lift at the hotel, I find myself being introduced to Monica Bellucci. I am stunned. Along with Gong Li, she must be the most beautiful actress currently working. I feel faint as she is crushed against me while the lift descends, all too quickly.

The restaurant is full of Hollywood people, some of whom I vaguely recognise, but can't pin down a single name. I suppose this would be easy if I lived in Los Angeles, as I'd always be bumping into film people. This is a move I've resisted. Not that I particularly dislike LA, in fact I enjoy being there. I think it would be a mistake to live in a place where virtually everyone is connected with the film industry. I don't really want to be cut off from everyday life. All the same, Sydney is a bit out of the mainstream, though with email I guess no one really knows where anyone else is anyway. The English director,

Michael Apted, told me once that without living in Los Angeles it's not possible to get the plum directing jobs.

15th May 2005

Long walk this morning down to the old town. Still attractive. Must've been gorgeous in the 1920s or 30s. There are some posters along the front for *The Contract*. Quite well designed, especially considering we haven't shot a foot of film. Avi Lerner is trying to sell the movie before it's made — standard practice, though I'm told the buyers are more wary these days and want to see a few scenes at least. They won't put up money just on the basis of a couple of star names and a director. J.D. Zeik will go into orbit if he finds out about the posters as he isn't credited on them as a writer. That credit goes to the original writers, Steve Katz and John Darrouzet, who I've never met and who were off the film before I came on board.

17th May 2005

Lunch with Eline De Kat, who was once my opera agent, but now works for Monte Carlo opera. A very bright Dutchwoman, who doesn't seem to have much luck with men. I think she's too quick-witted and too forthright. She has a friend with her, an American classical pianist. This woman tells me, at length, that George Bush is a business partner of Osama Bin Laden and that he collaborated with him in the World Trade Center tragedy! Also the Bali bombing. She is a little vague about what Bush had to gain from all this, and when I say this behaviour, if true, makes him one of the great all-time villains of history, she replies that this is indeed the case — 'In Europe everyone knows Bush was behind the World Trade Center, only Americans choose not to believe it'. I've heard this viewpoint many times in Los Angeles, but find it impossible to accept. Am I just an old conservative? Naïve? Bush certainly makes me cringe almost every time he speaks, but I find it hard to cast him in the role of a ruthless mass murderer and traitor.

18th May 2005

Pat Duggan has now turned up in Cannes, as cheerful and optimistic as ever. Claims he will have all the money for *Curlow Creek* by the end of June. He insists Bob Yari will put up a substantial proportion, though the letter he showed me from Yari was so carefully phrased it could mean anything. Pat is furious that Josh Maurer talked to Yari's people in LA (who told Josh they had not heard of the project) as this was 'damaging'. I said I didn't see how it could be. If Yari's company is interested, mentioning the film isn't going to cause it to collapse. Pat has now threatened legal action against Josh, who is bewildered by all this.

Evidently Bob Yari is staying in this hotel, right across the hall from me. I suggest to Pat that this might be a good time to introduce us so we can discuss *Curlow Creek*. Oddly, inexplicably, Pat resists the suggestion.

Vincent De Ville also appears in the lobby of The Carlton. Despite his claims, he hasn't produced the finance for *Fever*. He travels the world relentlessly and has apartments in Budapest and Los Angeles. Where does he get his income? He talks vaguely about some sort of cable TV deal in Hungary. Must be profitable. At least he's personable and amusing. Seems to speak most known languages with total fluency.

Dinner with Aurelio, his family and a group of Spanish buyers for one of his films at Moulin de Mougins — a great restaurant. Even the starters were around 100 euros and Aurelio didn't blanch at a 300 euro bottle of wine.

22nd May 2005

Back in London. Don't know what was resolved with Aurelio for *I Kill*. He said he'd get in touch with Tim Prager but I didn't sense much enthusiasm. I think I somehow made the wrong impression.* Maybe he expected me to

---

* Probably correct. I've never heard from Aurelio again.

be more effusive, and I probably should've made more of an effort. I'm aware that I often strike producers as being very low key, which they can interpret as lack of interest. Also, I know it's true that I'm not as enthusiastic about *I Kill* as I was about, say, *Wilberforce* or *Miss Potter*, even though I think it would make a good thriller.

Working since returning from Cannes on rewrite of *The Contract* with Tim Prager. I think it's improving; it could hardly get any worse. Tim has come up with a few plot twists. Might add a bit of interest for the audience.

A wonderful production of *Death of a Salesman* with a charismatic Brian Dennehy in the main role. At the beginning, a door onto the set wouldn't open. Dennehy pushed on it for a few moments then announced to the audience that this wasn't part of the play and he was going offstage so they could fix the door and begin again. The play is powerful, but with some strange moments. A long explanation from the wife about the salesman's problems seems to lay out the entire theme and plot in one chunk. I assume Arthur Miller thought the theme may be missed by the audience unless it was spelt out. There's great resistance to making cuts in plays. Quite right in general, but a lot of issues that were new at the time of writing are now familiar and explanations are often superfluous. A little trimming wouldn't go astray. I've seen some Shaw revivals that would've benefited from half an hour being removed. Eugene O'Neill plays could be cut by half or, better still, abandoned altogether.

A Woody Allen film, *Melinda and Melinda*. Very cleverly written, with the same central character and same scenes seen from a comic and then a tragic point of view. I like virtually all Woody Allen films, even the total flops. They always strike me as being so well thought out. His style is highly personal but he doesn't just trot out the same material. The subjects and characters are quite varied.

Tim Prager tells me that Aurelio was in touch re *I Kill* but didn't even offer as much as he gets for a one-hour BBC TV show.

24th May 2005

Back to Bulgaria. This time to begin pre-production on *The Contract*. Trish, my assistant, has lined up some places for me to rent. I don't want to stay in a hotel for months. I settle on a flat on the top floor of a run-down building. Although the staircase smells of dog and cat pee, the flat is large and has been restored in a modern/ dreadful style. Why do people put marble tiles on bathroom floors? The first time I had a shower I stepped out and skidded across the room, slamming into the wall on the far side. At least I can set up the stereo and play music full blast without anyone complaining. There is even a gym on a mezzanine floor so I have no excuses not to keep up with the exercises that my personal trainer

(Con, from Sydney) insists I do every day without fail. It's boring, but I have to keep fit. Every film is about a year's work, so I have to pass a complicated medical. When I look around at some of the clapped-out directors still working I can't imagine how they got through those things. Maybe they were so valuable to the financiers that they'd take the risk; just let them go ahead and direct without insurance. I don't think I'm in this category. If the doctors don't pass me, I'll be out and some perfect specimen will take over.

30th May 2005

In Bulgaria for nearly a week. Still wrestling with the final version of the script. Tim Prager has done wonders with the plot — at least we now have one. There is a bit too much dialogue, some of it repetitive, so I'm paring this down. Towards the end there are still a couple of scenes — the crossing of the ravine, the shoot out in the cabin — which are going to be difficult to make plausible, despite Tim's amendments. It might help when I tailor them to the locations, which are still to be found.

Went to a José Carreras concert in the old Communist 'Palace of Culture'. Four thousand people present. Great to see Carreras live, though he was amplified.

Deal now done with André Fleuren.* At last. I know the producers would like me to use a Bulgarian cameraman for the second unit,† but I've resisted. The schedule is tight and I can't risk having second unit footage that doesn't work, or doesn't match that shot by the first unit. With André, I know it'll be perfect. He'll follow my storyboards precisely, but imaginatively. On other films, pre-André, I had second unit footage shot that was useless. On the totally unmemorable *King David*, the second unit filmed for six weeks and I was unable to use a single shot. Stylistically, it looked like it was from a different film.

Dinner with Mark Egerton and his daughter, Lucy, who are still working on *The Black Dahlia*. Coming back late from dinner we walked past a restaurant where Brian De Palma and his producer were still eating. Their drivers were waiting outside — although they'd been on call since early morning — to drive them all of 100 yards back to their hotel.

Email to say Discovery Channel have rejected ALL of my ideas for the documentary about modern Australia. In retrospect, Beyond should've had the treatment approved before we shot anything.

---

* Australian–Dutch cameraman. I wanted him for second unit photography/ director.

† A second unit picks up footage, often action scenes, or inserts for action scenes, that the first unit doesn't have time to film. As films have become more elaborate, and audiences more demanding, second units often work for the entire shoot, paralleling the first unit, or doing 'pick up' shots that the first unit missed.

Hard to credit that Discovery want nothing but the usual Aussie stuff — outback drunks, road trains, crocodile hunters and surf carnivals. I'm sure it'll turn out well in any case. They've had so much experience producing for TV. I can't say I'm sorry. I don't much enjoy committee film-making — which is really what I'd plunged into — no matter how pleasant all the collaborators are. So nice to have producers like Richard Zanuck (*Driving Miss Daisy*), Sue Milliken (*Black Robe, Paradise Road*) and Dino De Laurentiis (*Crimes of the Heart*) whose attitude is, 'You're the director. You direct.' On *Daisy*, Zanuck was convinced that the final scene in the old folks home wouldn't work, as it seemed so quiet, so restrained, but then just said to me, 'I've hired you to direct it, I won't override your creative decisions.' Luckily, I was right for once! The scene worked.

2nd June 2005

Been working for six days on the script polish of *The Contract*. Streamlining Tom Pragers additions. Finally finished it tonight. Just hope they like it.

Met a beautiful Turkish–Australian actress, Dana Flynn, who has flown in from Istanbul. She's been told, it seems, there are roles available in the film. There is nothing for her, except maybe a small part as a TV reporter. She must be the girlfriend of one of the producers. She 'wants to live in LA' and thinks *Kill Bill* is a great film. Told me she has an IQ over 140. Why do so many actors feel obliged to tell everyone how intelligent they are? I suspect it's because they are in such a trivial occupation, one which often provides such lavish financial rewards and leads to so much undeserved adulation, that a bit of self-aggrandisement is necessary for self-esteem. They are denying to themselves that it's just their physical beauty that has been responsible for their success — though this must be the case 90% of the time.

Boaz Davidson is adamant about not using the African–American girl in the role of the hiker, despite my pleading. The second choice, Emily Deschanel, is now in a TV show and not available. I'll send them the tape of the American girl, Megan Dodds, I saw in the play in London.

7th June 2005

Dante Spinotti arrives for a location survey. He must've agreed to the (low) fee. It'll be my first film without Peter James as cameraman for ten feature films. Dante was probably influenced by the fact that he can easily fly over to his place in Italy from here. Just an hour or so.

Mike Scherer is here now, too. A 6 foot 7 stunt arranger from Canada, who I contacted some months ago after seeing his work in the Canadian film *Screamers*. Tells me he has a 14-year-old son who is already 6 foot 3.

In a van, we all travel out to the mountain locations in pouring rain. Landslides on the mountain roads. Some are nearly blocked. Rivers have risen, some towns are being evacuated. Naturally, everyone tells me this is not usual for summer in Bulgaria.

An email from a colleague of Rich Cowan's who is doing a film in Canada with John Cusack — says Cusack is totally mad. Hard to get him on set and he's endlessly crabby and argumentative!*

The street outside my apartment has dozens of bookstalls. Not much use to me as the books are nearly all in Bulgarian. There are a few dog-eared ones in English, most of them printed on cheap paper with a faint typeface, during the Communist era. There are also a group of furtive men who have piles of bootleg DVDs. I went through a bundle of these, then picked out a couple. For some reason (the police?) they're not available on the spot. The seller signals to a glabrous youth standing nearby, who dashes off, then returns about 15 minutes later with the discs.

Three times today I am approached by young(ish) men in conservative grey suits and carrying a briefcase. First

---

* Luckily, this behaviour, if accurately reported, did not carry over to *The Contract*. John was around half an hour late every day, but otherwise very professional and pleasant.

Australian second unit cameraman, André Fleuren, and Italian director of photography, Dante Spinotti, in Bulgaria on location for *The Contract*.

they ask for the time. Once I've stopped and told them they press a business card into my hand that offers sensual delights with young ladies.

8th June 2005

Saw one of the bootleg films, *Modigliani*—a Europudding film with Andy Garcia, written and directed by Mick Davis. It's well done, probably a bit too long, but I've not seen a film about painters which portrayed them or their work so convincingly — except the one about Artemisia Gentileschi.* All the paintings in the film look superb — and all done, I think, by contemporary painters. Usually these scenes let down the movie. If Piero della Francesca really painted as badly as he seemed to in *The English Patient* he'd never have achieved fame. I know that reproducing these works is terribly difficult. It's when some modern painter tries to reproduce some master that you realise just how brilliant, how skilful, the original artist was.

I've never heard of this Modigliani film (there was a French one made some years ago with Gérard Philipe and Anouk Aimée), so call my London casting director, Jeremy Zimmerman, who I noticed had a credit on it. He tells me the director is a Scotsman, the film was shot in Romania a couple of years ago and, to the best of his

---

* *Artemisia* (1997), directed by Agnès Merlet.

knowledge, has not been released anywhere. A shame as it's passionate and compelling. Why wouldn't it get shown? Probably categorised as an 'art' film by distributors and its appeal assumed to be limited.

9th June 2005

Spent all day going through the script with department heads. Rich Cowan has broken it down and tells me it's impossible to shoot the film in 50 days, which seems to be the figure the producers want. There is too much action and the mountain and forest locations mean we'll have a lot of travelling. He thinks 56 days is a possibility IF we recast the young (13) boy in the role of John Cusack's son. Because of the American Screen Actors Guild rules, we'll often have him for only four hours filming a day. He's in most scenes, so we'd never get through the schedule even in 56 days. The solution, I'm told, is to find a boy in London, as he'll be under the English equity rules, which are more flexible. Another factor affecting the schedule is that we have Morgan Freeman only for 30 days! The first 30 days!! So all of his scenes (nearly all with Cusack and the boy) have to be crammed into that time. Cusack is available for the whole shoot, *except* for the first nine days, because he's still shooting another film. It's all a nightmare. I hope we can find some convincing doubles.

The producers suggest that I cut the script to accommodate the 50-day schedule. I point out I've just cut 30 pages (!) and estimate the film now runs 95 minutes. It can't be any shorter.

11th June 2005

Weekend. I'm invited to a film festival in a town with an unpronounceable name (Székesfehérvár) about an hour from Budapest. Blanka, the Hungarian girl who runs the festival, said there would be a car at the airport to pick me up. No car shows up, then a phone call (thank God for mobiles) tells me there's been an accident somewhere or other and the car will be another hour. I have a few coffees and go through the script of *The Contract*, trying to work out the seemingly intractable cast availability problems. I am hoping the resourceful Rich Cowan can solve them. I can't think of anything.

The town holding the festival is quite beautiful and seems to have been thoroughly restored. I'm in a modern hotel, where most of the festival guests have been placed. Met Luis Mandoki — the Mexican director. He tells me his parents were European Jews who fled to Mexico, as so many did — I think it was one of the few countries that let them in. I know that Australia, disgracefully, had restrictions in the 1930s.

The first film I see is Mandoki's Mexican-made *Innocent Voices*, about children caught up in war in San Salvador. The story was told to him by one of the extras on a movie he was making. Very strong stuff. Done on a low budget in an ultra-realistic style. Wonderful acting from everyone involved. Quite different from the very Hollywood style films Mandoki has made in the USA.*

Awful Romanian film — *The Death of Mr Lazarescu* — took the main prize. Nearly three hours long and tedious. I left after 35 minutes. Central character had by then made four phone calls — all the same ... 'I'm sick, send an ambulance'.

Because I could only stay a couple of days I missed a lot of the films. Usually a good move at film festivals. But I did see the American film which won the top prize at Sundance, *Forty Shades of Blue*. Set in Memphis (though it had no atmosphere of that city), it seemed to me quite amateurish and confused. One of the actresses in the movie was present and as she didn't seem too enamoured of the film, I asked how it had won the Sundance prize. 'Oh,' she said, 'the director is a great friend of Sydney Pollack.' The Sundance award is almost a guarantee that the film is nonsense. Or am I just jealous because I've submitted films to the festival and never had one accepted?

---

* Such as *Message in a Bottle* (1999) and *When a Man Loves a Woman* (1994).

One of the festival people told me she was associated with the Taormina festival in Sicily. They'd invited Russell Crowe last year and he said he'd come if paid $350,000. Could this be true? All sorts of fanciful stories attach themselves to movie stars.

Blanka (who invited me to the festival) met John Cusack when he filmed *Max** in Budapest. She said he was rude to everyone . . . not good news. Still, I've often heard horror tales of actors and then experienced the reverse when I've worked with them. I was told by half a dozen people that Tommy Lee Jones (*Double Jeopardy*) was a nightmare, but he turned out to be rather shy, very pleasant, if somewhat reserved, and totally professional. Always arrived on time and didn't fluff one line during the entire shoot. Similarly, Sharon Stone (*Last Dance*) was very forthright, bright and witty. I suspect a lot of the biggest stars have reached their position partly, at least, because of their adaptability and sheer dedication.

13th June 2005

Morning. Back in Sofia. I go around the corner from my flat to a breakfast place in the next street. The entire

---

* An impressive film, written and directed by Menno Meyjes. Excellent performances from Cusack and Noah Taylor.

street is cordoned off with tape and there is no entry. The man from the café tells me that three men, all gangsters, were shot dead last night in the house opposite. I didn't hear anything. Maybe they used silencers in the true movie tradition.

At the production office I'm told that the line producer, Bob Misiorowski, is leaving the film. No idea why, and Bob isn't saying anything, but the rumour buzzing around is that the producers in LA want the budget reduced and, presumably, Bob isn't doing this. As I've no idea what the budget is (!) I can't comment and can't offer any suggestions.

It's likely that the fees paid to Morgan Freeman and John Cusack are so large that the producers have panicked and determined to spend as little as possible on the actual shooting of the film. This happens with a lot of American movies. The stars take huge fees, plus substantial chunks of the returns, so there is no alternative but to keep costs down on everything else — the fees of the supporting cast, crew fees, location fees, etc. Misiorowski has been with us on all the location surveys in the mountains (where almost the entire film is set) and is aware that if we don't use the most spectacular locations we can find we end up with a straight-to-DVD film (will we do this in any case?) so he supported me in my choices.

15th June 2005

Misiorowski leaves tomorrow. Still hasn't said anything about his reasons for going. Did he resign or was he pushed? Replacement producers have arrived. Les Weldon and Avi Lerner's brother, Danny. Les is smooth looking, rather like a TV newsreader.* Danny Lerner is tall, just like his brother Avi. He speaks a strange kind of English in which every word is undeniably an English word and is clearly pronounced, but the sentences are difficult to follow. (I later found that his emails have the same characteristic. One of the crew members forwarded me one of his emails with an enquiry about what it could mean. Again, every word was an English word, but the full sentences were incomprehensible). Between them, Les and Danny have produced and/or written and/or directed a large number of films, though they all seem to be DVD movies. I don't know any of the titles. Les has repeated what Avi Lerner has already told me — that we 'should be able to average 50 camera set-ups a day' as the Bulgarian crew are so fast! I can't believe the Bulgarian crews could be faster than American, British or Australian ones and 50 set-ups a day is an astonishing number. I don't think that many are done on TV shows, at least those with any pretension to quality. I've never done more than 20 and probably averaged only around 12 to 15.

---

* In fact, we cast him in that role in *The Contract*.

Les tells me we can't get Bill Smitrovich or Jonathan Hyde because of 'problems'. I'm sure the problems have to do with the actors' agents demanding fees the producers consider too high. Have to resolve this one as I can't go and find more actors at this stage.

Spent some days auditioning local actors for small roles. A few have worked in America and speak perfect English. Also, there are some American actors who have moved over here to take advantage of all the movies being shot in Eastern Europe. We also contact the American Embassy and some of their people, all clean cut, outgoing and fluent in Bulgarian, come in to audition for some of the smaller roles. A good-looking young lawyer is ideal for the man killed by Morgan Freeman near the beginning of the film.

The Bulgarian casting director, Mariana Stanisheva, is staggeringly beautiful. A welcome and not uncommon characteristic of Bulgarian women. She knows every actor in the country and even finds a man, from East Africa, who we can use to double Morgan Freeman.

Doing endless storyboards of the action scenes. A lot of work, especially as I have zero drawing skill and have to draw the images well enough for the various departments to understand the shots. On some of my early Hollywood films I had my storyboards redrawn by an artist, but found that although the images looked quite striking, often good enough to frame (I have framed some of those by an artist named Mentor Heubner), they didn't reflect the camera angles I wanted as clearly as my own childish efforts. I still do little more than stick figures but with the aid of a book on perspective anyone looking at my sketches can see if the camera is high or low, whether the lens is wide or long (I cheat here — I write down the millimetre lens I want to use) and the relative positions of the actors to one another.

18th June 2005

Back in London looking for a boy to play Cusack's son. Jeremy Zimmerman found about 12 who come and read for me. Three or four are very good, but the most appealing is the one with the least experience — Jamie Anderson — his father is a minister here in the American church. The family has been in London for some years, but Jamie has kept his American accent as he's been attending the American school. He tells me that they all moved back to Illinois a few years ago, but couldn't settle down in the USA after years in the UK, so just moved back again.

With kids it's best to find those who've had no acting coaching at all. Teachers seem to instill in them a set of contrived reactions, exaggerated facial expressions and pedantic speaking style. Without all this 'assistance' they behave quite naturally.

Adam, Vanessa and Cordelia are all staying in my London flat. Adam tells me he and Vanessa are getting married in January. I suspected I was about to hear this announcement, judging by the amount of time they've been spending together. I ask where they met. She was a student in his 'Introduction to Philosophy' course at Umass. Now she studies violin and plays in a string orchestra in Boston.

Adam has papers spread all over the dining room table. He is correcting the proofs of his translations for Penguin. With disbelief, he tells me that every word of the Greek text was misspelt, even though it was correct when he submitted it. I assume there aren't a lot of people around who can proofread classical Greek.*

I insist the curtains are drawn at night so the early morning sun doesn't fade any of the paintings. I've been collecting these, in a very modest way, since I was 15 and have seen a few fade away in bright light. I know that Adam, Cordelia and Vanessa all see my request as the raving of a senile old coot, judging by the exchanged looks with eye rolls that I manage to catch.

25th June 2005

Bulgaria. Still hunting for locations. Amazing that this company (NuImage) has made 40 films in Bulgaria but it hasn't occurred to anyone to set up a location department.

---

* Penguin have since published his translations of two Socratic dialogues, *Meno* and *Protagoras*.

No one has a clue about where to go to find the areas we need and no photographs have been collected. All we can do is drive out on the weekend with a list of what we need and hope we find something. The suggestion that we hire a helicopter for a day or two has been vetoed. This is a worry in itself as I was urged, while in LA, to put a lot of helicopter scenes in the film — 'including a crash' — as, I was assured, they have access to helicopters in Bulgaria. In fact, I find there are only two helicopters in the entire country (apart from an old Russian one the President uses) and they're used almost full time ferrying tourists to the Black Sea resorts. I pointed out this problem to the new producers and was then shown a mock-up helicopter made of wood. Needless to say this thing doesn't fly. It might be OK for a few shots from the outside, but the interior is useless as it doesn't have any detail.

At least the actors I wanted all seem to have come through. The deals have been done.

Pat Duggan calls. Insists he'll have the finance for *Curlow Creek* by the end of this month.*

Benjamin was supposed to arrive today, but the Bulgaria Air flight didn't leave Paris. I'm told it's the world's worst airline. Spoke to Benjamin, who is in a hotel with some minder from the airline. He seems OK.

---

* Now — 2007, mid-year, he still doesn't have it.

My daughter, Cordelia, camera operating on *The Contract*.

27th June 2005

This morning I find the Italian special effects crew have been sent home. (No consultation with me, needless to say.) This is worrying. We have a lot of action scenes — a car over a cliff, gunfights and a helicopter crash. How do we do this without specialists? I'm told that the Bulgarians have enough experienced people to be able to handle everything.

7th July 2005

Bombs went off in London a few hours ago, mostly on the underground, but one on a a bus. Thirty-seven reported dead so far. Al Qaeda suspected. Will this be pinned on George Bush? Adam, Vanessa and Rhoisin are in London and all near the explosions, but all OK. The bomb on the bus was only a few hundred yards from my apartment.

We start filming on Monday. Very few actors here yet. Morgan Freeman arrives tomorrow (Friday) and Cusack not until we've been filming a week or more. So much for the week's rehearsal I was originally promised.

A pre-shoot party at David Varod's, who has one eye and a pigtail and looks like Long John Silver. The story is he was in Mossad and got blown up. He held his face together and walked to a hospital. All the Israelis have had military training and are very tough. Someone told me that Avi Lerner trained the parachutists who took part in the Entebbe raid. David has a pretty Bulgarian girlfriend who is probably only in her twenties. She's been assigned to Herbert Pinter's art department as a set dresser. He isn't too happy. Says she isn't resourceful and doesn't even appear very interested in the job.

8th July 2005

I visit Morgan Freeman in the costume department where he is trying on the various suits and jackets he has to wear throughout the movie. He has few costume changes as he spends most of the movie walking through the forest with no alternative ensemblé. He is as relaxed and courteous as ever. I'm relieved when he says he's pleased with the script revisions. We've even kept him alive at the end as he suggested.

11th July 2005

Filming began today. For the first nine days we have to shoot everything without John Cusack, which means we start with some interior scenes with Morgan Freeman. The problem with this is that we will be shooting all our weather cover.* Once we move outdoors, which is the bulk of the film, we'll have no interiors to go to if the weather turns against us.

We shoot the long opening scene, ostensibly in a chic New York apartment. Herbert Pinter has done his usual thorough job and the paintings by Jeffrey Smart around the walls give it an eerie atmosphere. We cover the dialogue with two cameras — Dante operating one and Cordelia the other.

All seems to go OK. Morgan is as charismatic as always. A fairly easy scene to shoot — a group of men around a table, talking.

Day 1 of 56 is over.

The Contract is my 25th feature film.

---

* It is normal practise to keep interior scenes in reserve — and film them when bad weather prevents outdoor shooting.

EPILOGUE

Naturally, our Bulgarian summer turned out to be the wettest and coolest in Bulgarian history, in keeping with the law of nature which states that whenever a film company arrives on a location the weather pattern of centuries is to go into immediate reverse.

This was an irritating factor in a film that had more than 70% of its scenes taking place outdoors, and, as I've already mentioned, we had to shoot our weather cover in the first nine days because of John Cusack's unavailability. John was most co-operative and helpful once he did arrive. He had that wonderful knack that I so admire in actors of being able to give the impression that he's making up all the dialogue as he goes along. A further problem, though, was that someone with the production company (though no one stepped forward and took responsibility) told John he would only have to work a five-day week. Everyone else, including Morgan Freeman, worked a six-day week. This meant that some sequences, allegedly with John Cusack, were actually shot over the shoulder of a huge (as John is over 6 foot tall and powerfully built) non-English speaking Bulgarian lookalike.

A major difficulty was shooting all of Morgan's scenes in the 30 days allocated to us of the 50 or 56 day schedule — depending on whether we were observing the realistic schedule drawn up by the first assistant, Rich Cowan, or the fanciful one decided on without reference to the requirements of the script by the producers.

This meant we had to rush from location to location making sure we shot all of Morgan's close shots and, of course, anything with dialogue. For almost everything else, we could use our East African double, an amiable man, who, fortunately, bore a strong resemblance to Morgan (this would seem to be essential for doubles, but is not always the case — a friend of mine who made a film with Robert De Niro said that his double was more appropriate for Mickey Rooney) and was quite happy to be thrown into raging rivers and forced to climb down near-vertical cliffs in the (artificial, but nevertheless, wet) rain.

Considering that our special effects team had been dismissed before filming began, the various special effects sequences worked reasonably well. We imported two

identical American cars for our car-over-the-cliff
sequence (this is how Morgan Freeman ends up in the
river, handcuffed, and then meets up with hiking father
and son team John Cusack and Jamie Anderson; they
spend the rest of the movie in the woods, being pursued
by the remnants of Morgan's gang — exciting stuff), but
the stunt driver at our first attempt somehow missed his
markings on the road, with the result that a couple of
cleverly concealed cameras failed to film anything except
a patch of sky. I told the producers we'd have to film the
stunt again with car number 2, but was then told that the
car was unavailable as it was being used to ferry VIPs to
and from the airport! I had to make do with a car that
didn't match the first one. The editor, Mark Warner,
looked at the footage in disbelief and asked me if I
thought the audience would notice that the car had
shrunk about 7 feet and changed colour (from black to
grey) in mid-air.

Helicopters were a bigger problem. Because these are
in very short supply in Bulgaria we had no alternative but
to put them in digitally for a number of shots, although
for one key sequence we were able to hire one of the two
tourist choppers and have it hover over a mountain top
while we filmed. For the big crash sequence the
enterprising South African model maker (resident in
Bulgaria), Willie Botha, rigged up his wooden replica on
rails in the forest, ran a rope around a large tree, then, on
cue, had a truck (attached to the other end of the rope)

With John Cusack and Morgan Freeman on *The Contract*.

drive at high speed down the road. This caused the bogus helicopter to hurtle through the undergrowth, it's three-actor occupants looking suitably terrified. This wasn't particularly difficult for them as they'd all observed the Bulgarian crew laying bets on the stunt working.

The cast and crew certainly didn't seem to mind being in Bulgaria for months, although few of them had any idea where it was before actually arriving. When speaking to one of the actors on the phone, during the casting period, he said to me, 'It must be very cold there.' I replied that it was quite warm. He seemed confused and I realised he was mixing up Bulgaria with the Baltic States. He imagined we were filming somewhere near Finland, rather than a country adjoining Greece.

Having thrown off the killjoy Communist rulers, Bulgaria suddenly exploded with Western consumerism. Restaurants, nightclubs, coffee shops and boutiques are everywhere. Cast and crew members were overjoyed to meet the amazing number of young and gorgeous Bulgarian women who thronged the above establishments in their standard summer attire of see-through white slacks *sans* panties. Nearly all of these young women spoke excellent English — the reason being, I was told, that American movies are shown with subtitles, not dubbed into Bulgarian, so that just about everyone under 30 can chatter away with an American accent and American slang.

Romances developed, even a couple of marriages. The beautiful Bulgarian girls, it turns out, feel no compulsion to leave their country. Instead, their foreign-born husbands (American/South African/Israeli/Australian, etc) have to stay, where most of them find work in the film industry, now going through something of a boom because of the low costs, a factor which could change rapidly now that the country is part of the European Union. Further, these foreigners have to learn to speak Bulgarian (a Slavic language, akin to Russian) — something few of them seem to accomplish, though it seems to me that frequent repetition of the word *dobre* gives the illusion of fluency.

The biggest problem with the filming of *The Contract* was, as I predicted, the issue of the schedule. I simply could not complete the film in the 50 days the producers were so insistent was no problem. The reassessment of the situation after a couple of weeks filming never happened. Around Day 40 I was told that all action stopped on Day 50. No one was interested in my protestations that a number of major sequences would not be completed (including almost all of the helicopter shots) so the film would not be coherent. Judging by previous films made by the company, coherence was not a major objective.

Normally in such a situation a bond company steps in, appoints a supervisor, and sees that the shooting is completed to the extent that the film can be cut together. In this case, though, the bond company made it clear that they would not ride to the rescue. I was puzzled about their involvement in the production at all if they offered no assistance in this, the one situation in which they are often called upon.

Finally, I was given to understand that the final six days of filming, up to the 56 days I always insisted would be needed, could only proceed if I paid for it myself. Unwillingly, I had to take this course, there being no alternative — except that of a partially completed film released (even if only on DVD) with my name still attached as director.

A colleague said to me on the phone recently, 'It's all so stressful this business. I don't know how you can stand it.' But I don't find it so stressful, despite all the problems, all the conflicts. I could be in a boring job like my father had all his life. Instead I've travelled (and am travelling, I go to America to discuss new films in two days' time) the world and met all kinds of fascinating people. Made friends in at least a dozen countries. Above all, I've directed a lot of movies — something I wanted to do since I was five years old — and am very proud of many of them.

And all those other projects? *Walking Off the Map* (the one about George Mallory, the Everest climber), *Fever* (the one about the pioneering Hungarian doctor, Semmelweiss) and my own scripts — *The Women in Black*, *Curlow Creek* and *The Fortunes of Richard Mahoney*. All are still inching forward, or perhaps backward, in the search for finance and a cast. Sometimes I'm amazed that any films are made at all as it's so difficult to set them up, but hundreds are, every year. I'm sure that all but a few of the biggest studio films with the biggest stars and most commercially successful directors have the same kinds of problems I've discussed in this book. There are a lot of dedicated, not to say obsessed, producers and directors around who will fight to realise their pet projects long past the point where logic would tell them to quit and open up a bookshop or a market stall.

And the Chet Baker film? Does Josh Hartnett definitely want to do it? After the diary section covered in this book I somehow found time to write a new Chet Baker script. This involved months of research, but I was pleased with the result and sent it off to the producer, Pieter Kroonenburg, to forward to Josh. I heard nothing for months, then met Pieter for coffee in Los Angeles early in 2007. He assured me that Josh *is* still enthusiastic about the project but doesn't like my script at all. He prefers a revised script by Julie Allen, Pieter's partner. Further, he will only do the film if I don't direct.